*For Art - With admiration
and appreciation and with
every good wish —*

Jim Kinnear

*Art
2009*

THE MAN WHO
WORE THE STAR

*Real-time Perspectives
on a Business Leader's Changing World*

By James W. Kinnear

*With a Foreword by
Henry Rosovsky*

**The Business Council
of New York State, Inc.**

Albany, New York

ISBN 0-9715754-0-1

This book is printed on acid-free paper.

Printed in the United States of America.

Dedication

To Mary, my wife, without whose optimism, faith and fighting spirit this book's happy ending would not have occurred.

To the men and women of Texaco, whose skill, determination and unwillingness to accept defeat represent a model of courage in dealing with an "outrageous fortune," and who were able to reconstruct their company into a competitive powerhouse, bringing energy to the world and satisfaction to its shareholders.

Author's Note

The speeches contained herein are real, as-delivered versions of those that were made during a tumultuous period in the life of a great corporation. They tell the story of a business epoch and of a period in one company's history, which I hope will be useful to others. This book is a study of communication, of course, but it is also a study of business leadership in times of crisis and of change.

No proper names of most of the Texaco participants are used. I cannot, however, refrain from praising Alfred C. DeCrane, Jr. for the role he played in the drama described herein. Al was the Chairman of the Board of Texaco Inc. and a leading participant in all of these events. His leadership, wise counsel and ability to stand up to adversity were enormous assets. He was elected by the Board to begin his own successful tour as Chief Executive Officer on April 1, 1993.

Nor can I fail to recognize the hard work, dedication, and professional contribution provided over so many years by my assistant and friend Cathy Doherty. She not only was a loyal warrior in the battles recounted, but devoted hours to the organization of this account.

Our editor, David Shaffer, who in his other life is President of the Public Policy Institute of New York State, Inc., supplied his considerable editorial expertise and also his business acumen as a critical observer of this and other corporations coping with the changing fortunes of modern America.

THE MAN WHO WORE THE STAR

Real-time Perspectives on a
Business Leader's Changing World

By James W. Kinnear

Foreword

BY HENRY ROSOVSKY

Geyser University Professor Emeritus and
former Dean of the Faculty of Arts and Sciences,
Harvard University

In the 1950s, early in my career as a student of economic history, I became affiliated with the Research Center in Entrepreneurial History at Harvard University. Inspired by the seminal ideas of the famous Austrian economist Joseph A. Schumpeter, the Center's goal was to document and appreciate the role of the entrepreneur in the history of business: to focus on the innovator, on leadership, on the human being. Our success was mixed because analytical fashion was increasingly turning towards more impersonal forces, such as market structure, geography, and international relations.

Jim Kinnear's book once again convincingly demonstrates the centrality of human will, imagination, and courage in understanding business enterprises. That is why these vivid chapters are so valuable for those currently enrolled in business schools. They will be equally valuable to anyone interested in understanding the strength and resiliency of the American economy.

Jim led a great American oil company, Texaco, through and out of what was quite literally its darkest hour—when a haywire judgment in a Texas court set off a chain of events that forced his company into bankruptcy, and then into a near-death experience with speculators who wanted to take it over and break it up at fire-sale prices. When Jim retired in 1993 Texaco was in full recovery. Just eight years later this once-bankrupt enterprise yielded over $35 billion for its shareholders, upon its merger with Chevron. His leadership has passed the test of time.

After Jim stepped down, a number of his friends—myself among them—repeatedly pestered him to find a way to pass on some of the key lessons that he had learned in his career about leadership and about crisis management. This book, at long last, is his answer to that request.

Typically of Jim, the approach he takes here is singularly innovative, bold, and even a little risky. For he offers both his own considered, post-retirement thoughts on the challenges facing corporate leadership, and source material that students of business may use to measure what he says now against what he said then. Each chapter contains his current commentary on a key topic, ranging from the takeover fight to environmental protection. But each also includes the actual text of speeches on these topics, as he delivered them when he was under the burden of leadership. The student of business can learn not only what this retired CEO says now, with the benefit of hindsight—but can also read and assess the words Jim used to exercise leadership when he was actually in the line of fire. Thus we are offered, literally, a real-time perspective on how he dealt with his challenges.

Many of us, I suspect, might prefer to approach an audience today with only our own, ex-post-facto thoughts on what we did and why we did it, hoping that the things we actually said at the time will not get subjected to particularly close retrospective scrutiny. Jim Kinnear, however, is taking the risk.

His speeches hold up rather well, I think; they offer us a clear window into the mind of a corporation, and its leader, at a critical time in its history. They may not be masterpieces of prose; typically speeches contain a series of ideas expressed without the careful wording of an essay. Speeches must be delivered with passion, with humor, with body language, gestures, asides and pauses—few of which can appear on the printed page. I encourage the reader, therefore, to use his or her imagination, to picture the event, be it before a downcast and scared workforce, an angry and confused group of shareholders, a hostile adversary, or a sympathetic group of friends. When this real-time dimension is seen in the speeches, they come to life and let us have some understanding of the challenges faced by CEOs in their daily lives.

In some cases these speeches do not have quite the level of candor of the contemporary essays with which Jim introduces them. But there is a good reason for that. As a tenured faculty member at a research university, absolute freedom of speech has been not only a constitutional right for me, but a constantly exercised stock-in-trade; from an educational point of view, the more controversial, the more thought-provoking, the more original, the more colorful, the better. After all, I was speaking only for myself. A corporate CEO, on the other hand, lives under the same constitutional right, but has other constraints; he must simultaneously deal with employees, customers, regulators, stockholders, foreign and domestic governments and with his own legal department, and all of these constituencies appear to have different and changing agendas. The CEO speaks not only for himself, but also for the entire corporation.

Even with those constraints, however, I believe that both the speeches, as well as the accompanying essays, provide valuable insights into the nuances of corporate governance, the demands of crisis management, the realities of politics and economics, and the critical nature of oil supply to the world in the 21st Century.

For those reasons, I was very happy to accept Jim's invitation to supply a foreword for his book.

I have known Jim Kinnear as a traveling companion and friend for over 20 years. We have shared experiences on two major corporate boards and have seen some outstanding directors who truly have a sense of strategy, who have an ability to ask penetrating questions in a non-accusatory way, and who do their homework for the good of the shareholders. (We have also known others with less ambitious goals.) I have tried to use our long association to convince Jim that academics are not necessarily hopeless when it comes to practical matters. My success in this endeavor remains uncertain.

I have found Jim to be absolutely honest and trustworthy, except when he is describing himself. He will look you in the eye and tell you that he is the only person he has ever met who has no ego, and he will tell you that he is a farm boy from western Pennsylvania. Both statements are false. No one could have successfully existed in his line of work without considerably more than the average degree of self-confidence (read, "ego"). And his youthful experience with farming consisted solely of raising 50 chickens with the daily assistance of his family's hired man.

Yet the truth about Jim is better than his own fiction. In 1946 he chose to pursue his higher education under the competitive rigors of the U.S. Naval Academy, rather than accept admission to the more ivied halls that were open to him. It was a decision rooted in love of country, and he has remained a loyal, active and supportive alumnus. He spent some 30 months in the combat zone in Korea as a junior officer in the U.S. Navy. The decoration of which he is most proud was received during the Korean War for saving the life of a drowning paratrooper and for trying (in vain) to resuscitate two others. These early experiences with death at first hand, he has said, "made me grow up in a hurry." In fact, the Navy marked him for life. His shoes are always shined and his clothes are worn with the neatness and elegance of Dress Blues. (It should be added that I have never had the opportunity to observe Jim with his beloved dogs on his farm in Virginia, but I would bet that his shoes would still be shined.) More to the point, Jim projects what I can only call "command presence," and the chapters that follow show that he truly was captain of Texaco.

Upon the completion of his military service, Jim joined Texaco. Born in Texas in 1902, the company had created for itself a colorful history of success in the international oil business, involving exploration, production, transportation, refining and marketing of oil. But in 1985, in a lawsuit over its acquisition of the Getty Oil Co., Texaco suffered an appalling defeat in a Houston District Court, a decision characterized by The New York Times as "reminiscent of what passes for justice in small countries run by colonels in mirrored sunglasses."

Thus Jim's tenure as Texaco's CEO began, in 1986, in the throes of corporate emergency, which forged the experience in crisis management that forms a central part of this book. But there is still more here for the student of business. For example, Jim has made a careful study of competition—a very useful practice for anyone in the oil business. In the chapters that follow one will see how he compared his company to competitors (not always favorably) and what he set out to do about the deficiencies. He will lead us through other challenges: issues concerning the environment, about which he cares so deeply; the ethical questions which confront a company operating in 150 jurisdictions; and the ever-changing world of technology—what does the CEO need to know and how does he get to know it? Jim and I have been in action together in the world of corporate governance and of shareholder relations; from these associations and from his long experiences on and with Texaco's board the chapters on corporate governance and on shareholder relations are drawn.

The author of this book is not your stereotypical oil man. We do not necessarily associate this profession with environmental concerns or sophisticated discussion of ethical practices. And how many oil men quote Shakespeare, Julius Caesar, and discuss the strategies of the Spanish Armada? Most probably, the stereotype is flawed, but Jim would stand apart from the crowd in any profession.

For Jim Kinnear, I know, retirement was bittersweet. He loved his company and he loved his job, and hated to leave each. But the time had come to practice leadership in other ways. The creation of this book is but one of them.

Readers in my generation will recall a Texaco advertising slogan of long standing: "You can trust your car to the man who wears the star." Jim Kinnear wore the Texaco star with pride and with commitment. You can trust him. Listen carefully, and you will hear the real voice of a great corporation and a wise leader as the company struggled for its own survival, and as it competed to bring energy to the world.

Cambridge, Massachusetts
November 2000

Introduction

A Tuesday afternoon in Houston, November 19, 1985, sticks in my mind as the loneliest moment of my life. After an 18-week charade, a jury in a dingy, upper-story courtroom had pronounced what seemed like a death sentence for Texaco—a $10.5 billion verdict I knew could drain the life out of the company to which I and thousands of others had dedicated our careers.

As Vice Chairman of Texaco's Board of Directors and the company's representative at the scene, I walked out of the courtroom to face the news media. Alone in front of a battery of TV cameras, the best I could come up with was a promise that we would appeal, and a statement of faith in the ultimate fairness of the U.S. judicial system.

That faith was sorely tried by subsequent events. So, too, were the people of Texaco—a proud name that has always stood for integrity and quality in more than 150 countries around the world. Yet we came through the crisis, and in the process we grew stronger.

As I look back over these events, and many others during my nearly forty years in the oil business, the last twenty-seven of which were spent as a senior officer of the corporation, I am reminded of one of the many truths I learned from my mother: "The days are long, but the years are short."

In a few short years we faced tremendous challenges, to which we were forced to respond by making major changes in our business. To drive those changes required real leadership.

The demands of leadership, in turn, required me to speak to thousands of employees, shareholders and others interested in our company. With our company's fundamental existence at stake, our leadership had to be based on fundamentals, as well. The basic principles of optimism, competitive excellence, ethical behavior, planning and persistence all resonated with our audiences, and proved to be the roadmap out of our crisis.

This experience in one corporation's darkest days taught me lessons about leadership and communication that turned out to be useful, as well, outside of crisis situations—in addressing issues as varied as environmental policy, international relations, and corporate governance.

Good communication is an essential element of good leadership. It connects through shared values. It focuses on principles. And whatever the topic, good communication is direct, honest, and candid. You must always play it absolutely straight; your credibility is a priceless asset. You must keep a clear head; unless your thinking is clear in your own mind, you're certainly not going to be able to communicate it clearly. And, frankly, you must be willing to repeat yourself; you must deliver your fundamental messages to a number of different audiences—and more than once to some audiences—if you want to have an impact.

This book is an open window on the real-time words and actions of one company and its people, facing challenges that provide test-tube examples of these principles. It is offered in the hope that future generations of leaders might learn something from our struggles.

For leadership is a quality—and a skill—upon which much depends.

What is leadership? Can it be taught? Is it simply a reflection of outside events—that is, do leaders make history, or does history make leaders? How is leadership learned? What role do our moral values—our ethics—play in the exercise of leadership?

The word "leadership" may at first conjure up the image of Henry V at Agincourt: "Once more into the breach, dear friends, once more." Or we may think of Winston Churchill: "We will never surrender." Or of General McAuliffe at Bastogne replying to a surrender offer: "Nuts!"

But the practice of leadership that is illustrated in this book is not that of the field of battle. Leadership occurs in everyday life, in the classroom, in the vestry meeting, at the board table, and in the family. Whatever the venue, the effective leader is driven not by the hope of personal gain, but by the dream of success for the enterprise and all those who depend upon it.

Leaders exist to get groups of people to pursue and achieve common objectives. They must persuade both by words, and by example. The objectives may be the group's, or the leader's own. Or they may be determined by higher authority—an important point, since leaders exist throughout an organization. As Napoleon said, "each soldier has in his knapsack the baton of a marshall."

Leaders are not afraid to bare their souls. And they must show their human frailties—for leaders are not infallible. Leaders must have self-confidence; but self-confidence is strengthened, rather than weakened, by making mistakes and then having to clean them up.

In a career spent mostly in operations, I have made some beauties. And in the oil business there are few "little" mistakes, even for the most junior employee. As the supervisor of operations for a subsidiary in Puerto Rico, I was asked one day to dispatch a barge-load of diesel fuel to the electric plant on the nearby island of Vieques. We had a new terminal superintendent, so I elected to help him with the loading. We "followed the book"—at least most of it—and flushed the barge out with water before loading it up with diesel fuel for the generators. Our tug took the barge to Vieques and we pumped the fuel ashore. After about an hour, all the generators shut down and turned out every light on the island. Unfortunately, although we had washed out the barge, we had neglected the manifold, which was still full of the contents from a previous run—molasses. "Diesel Dulce!" (sweet diesel), screamed the headlines in the local press. I had a big to-do list after that one: retrieve the fuel, resupply with uncontaminated product, line up an emergency generator, deal with insurance companies, and worry about what I would do if I lost my job.

At the height of one crisis in the Texaco takeover battle, a newspaper reporter asked me, "What was the worst mistake you ever made?" My answer, which was both true and (I thought at the time) appealingly modest: "Lord, I have made so many mistakes I can't single out one." Well, that quote turned out to be *another* mistake! Literally within hours, my words were printed in six-inch type in newspapers across the country, in ads placed by my opponent at the time: "Kinn-ear says he has made so many mistakes he can't remember them!"

Yet willingness to dare, to take risks, is essential to true leadership. And you cannot dare if you are afraid to make mistakes. Nor can you second-guess yourself, or lie awake worrying about your decisions; enough people will find fault with you by themselves, without your help.

Vital, as well, is a willingness to listen to others, to keep an open door for new perspectives and new ideas. Leadership also requires a willingness to walk through the doors that others keep open to you— to stand squarely and state your case without flinching, whether you think it will be popular and well-received, or not.

In the chapters that follow, speeches I made as a senior executive are presented as real-time windows into the hearts and minds of the leadership of a corporation as it dealt with difficult situations. We were faced with the necessity of re-energizing a demoralized company, explaining inexplicable events to the investing public, rallying public and political support, and simultaneously producing oil at a profit.

In my mind each of these speeches represents a key milepost; in this book, each is preceded by a background narrative that places the message in context.

Not every speech was a response to corporate warfare or some other crisis, of course. There were many other issues of concern to us in those years. One of the lessons to be taken from these accounts is that the ability to keep several balls in the air at once is essential for business success—as it is for personal satisfaction.

It is essential to be able to think clearly about, and arouse interest in, topics that do not represent an obvious crisis; indeed, often that is the only way to keep some problems from *becoming* a crisis. Thus such topics as the environment, regulatory reform, community interests, ethics, trade policy, international relations, and the need to pass on the torch to new leaders in their turn, all find a place in this retrospective.

It is also essential to be able to communicate to a range of audiences, in a variety of different circumstances, and for a number of different purposes. The speeches here were sometimes made to motivate, sometimes to entertain—to teach, to thank, to inform. Some were made to company employees, several to business schools, some to professional organizations, others to annual meetings or to meetings convened for special purposes. Some were recorded, some televised and some mailed to a larger audience. Some were delivered from notes; others were carefully written out and edited in advance.

Few individuals will be mentioned by name in this brief history. That does not mean that they did not exist. As the speeches will suggest, there were heroes and villains enough to fill the stage of any opera. There was bravery and sacrifice, corruption and venality, invention and vision, greed and cowardice. But the details of individual deeds and misdeeds—however interesting, heroic or outrageous they may have been—are, in this context, less important than our response to them.

Even more important, the speeches assembled in this collection seem to me to offer recurring themes that transcend the immediate crisis or the topic being addressed. These themes—optimism, competitive excellence, ethical standards, concern for people, protection of the environment—will all continue to play a part in the careers of the managers of today and tomorrow, whatever the specific challenges they face.

CHAPTER

1

Corporate Crisis

1971 was truly a watershed year in the history of the oil industry. U.S. oil production finally peaked out, after a century of growth. The Texas Railroad Commission could no longer control the balance between supply and demand in the world, as it had for many years. The power to do so had moved to OPEC, the Organization of Petroleum Exporting Countries, which Saudi Arabia and Venezuela had formed in 1960 with the objective of wresting pricing decisions out of the hands of the oil companies.

Following this fundamental shift in power, the behavior of the producing countries could be expected to shift—and it did. Nationalization (often euphemistically referred to as "participation") became the order of the day. This change in production asset control started in Venezuela, and was followed in various forms by Libya, Kuwait, Iran, the United Arab Emirates, Saudi Arabia, and other OPEC members. The Arab oil embargo of 1973 created the fear, if not the reality, of shortages around the world. Long lines to buy gasoline appeared at service stations in the U.S.—because the U.S., unlike the developed countries in Europe and the Far East, elected to rely on government edicts (in the form of allocation and price controls), rather than on the free market, to allocate available petroleum. The Iranian Revolution of 1978 further strengthened the politicization of global oil markets.

After the political upheavals, controls and realignments of the 1970s, the oil industry found itself in a different economic environment in the early 1980s. We faced high crude oil prices, and the expectation of even higher ones. We saw an historic frenzy in exploration activity in the U.S. and around the world. There was a string of mergers and acquisitions in the industry, fueled by the availability of junk-bond financing, by the expectation of ever higher oil prices, by the increase in exploratory costs, and by the perceived shortage of prospective acreage. Although many of these perceptions later proved to have been wrong, they all had their impact in the 1980s.

Against this backdrop, in early January 1984 Texaco was invited by the Getty Oil Company, by Getty's investment banker and by its largest stockholder to make an offer to acquire that company. Texaco made an offer, which was accepted in writing by Getty and by its largest stockholder.

But Pennzoil, which had been in negotiation to buy a minority position in Getty, promptly sued Texaco. The suit charged us with "tortious interference with contract"—a contract Pennzoil purportedly had with Getty. This "contract" consisted solely of a Getty/Pennzoil press release announcing "an agreement in principle, subject to shareholder approval and definitive agreements," neither of which conditions was ever satisfied.

Though our differences seemed irreconcilable, we initially tried to resolve them out of court. But we were unable to do so (a fact that, with hindsight, haunts me to this day, in view of the severe consequences of the case). A jury trial commenced in State Court 151, Houston, Texas, beginning on July 8, 1985.

As Vice Chairman of Texaco's Board of Directors, I attended the trial. In retrospect the result seems to have been foreordained. The first trial court judge, who later became physically incapacitated, had accepted a significant campaign contribution from Pennzoil's counsel.* Texaco objected, but this trial court judge wrote that "mere bias and prejudice are not grounds for recusal." The succeeding trial court judge, who had been visiting the court several weeks before being selected to serve, later said "there is a good chance that perhaps I may

---

* *Disclosure statement filed by the judge on July 13, 1984, with the Harris County Clerk in Texas.*

have read the cases wrong and not have applied it correctly, and as I said, you know, it was my first experience in trying to analyze New York law after I had been 46 years with Texas."*

Every day the testimony made clear that there never had been a contract between Getty and Pennzoil; in fact, the judge's final charge to the jury never mentioned the word "contract." But no matter. On November 19 the jury came up with an award of $7.5 billion in compensatory damages, plus $3 billion in punitive damages.

Settlement talks between the parties had begun in 1985 and continued in 1986. But the gap between what Texaco was willing to offer and what Pennzoil was asking for obviously escalated as a result of this huge jury verdict.

On October 23, 1986, the Board of Directors elected me President and Chief Executive Officer of Texaco Inc. effective January 1, 1987. As one wag put it at the time, "The good news is, you got the job. The bad news is, you got the job."

I did not agree with the wag. I was absolutely sure that the U.S. system of justice would at some point put right this nefarious legal wrong, and that Texaco could be returned to a position of leadership in the international oil business.

There were only three problems: a $10.5 billion judgment with no clear path for an appeal; a demoralized and frightened workforce; and a worldwide enterprise that needed to do $150 million in business a day, mostly on credit.

Nor was our enterprise in perfect shape, even before the court case. The decade of the 1970s had not been a happy one for Texaco. An inefficient 50-state marketing system and 11 refineries, mostly of less than optimum size, had been frozen in place in the U.S. by the price and allocation controls. The company began addressing this problem in the early 1980s, but was behind its competitors in doing so. Likewise, exploration and production activities and exploration acreage had been allowed to deteriorate.

These were the thoughts that occupied my mind when, between Christmas and New Year's Eve 1986, I sat down with a yellow pad to write what I called "the vision speech."

---

* *Address to the Los Angeles County Bar Association, April 2, 1986.*

I knew that as soon as I took over as CEO, I had to address our employees—to arouse them, to reassure them, and to provide an optimistic view of the future. I prepared a talk that was, in the corporate context, an outrageous speech. And it was meant to be outrageous—to challenge our company to do much better, even as we were comforting ourselves in our hour of trial. I delivered it to groups of company employees, first in New York, and then in rapid succession in Los Angeles, Denver, Houston, Delaware City and London.

MILEPOST: JANUARY 1987

A Vision for Texaco, As a New CEO

New York, Los Angeles, Denver, Houston, Delaware City and London

———

I've never been an advocate of New Year's Resolutions. They don't seem to last through the end of January. Mine sometimes don't even make it past the Rose Bowl! But as we begin this New Year, I'm going to make an exception—because I want to make sure we make it a year to remember. We have a new management team and new challenges. It is time to take stock of ourselves: to ask together who we are and what we want to be—what we want this great company to be.

As most of you know, Texaco is my life's work—and I know most of you feel the same way. We came here to make a difference—to count for something in our lifetimes. Texaco has always been a name spoken with pride. We've written that name large all over this country, and all over the world. We're entitled to be a little sentimental about it at times—and this may be one of those times.

As I undertake my own new responsibilities, I want to share some thoughts with you—the real operators of this company. I know many of you personally, and over the years I've acquired from you a great and enduring faith in the rare quality of the people who make Texaco. This quality is one of the true foundations of this company, and it's on this foundation that we are going to build our future.

Some people may look at Texaco and see a lot of hardware — the pumps and tanks and walls and ships that carry the Star.

But when I look at Texaco, the first thing I see is the richness of our people and their potential. Without our people, the hardware means nothing. You are the ones who make Texaco work.

I know the roller coaster we've been riding has made it hard at times to focus on goals that extend much beyond holding on through the next twist and turn. Sometimes we all must feel that long-range planning means the next half-hour.

And that's been an industry-wide problem as well. The dramatic swings in the price of crude oil have had a tremendous impact on our ability to make the sound, long-range investment decisions that are pivotal to our competitiveness.

We've had to face added uncertainties created by the Pennzoil lawsuit. I'm not going to dwell on that today, except to say that my confidence in the rightness of our position is unshakable.

The current court judgment is insane. But our country and our legal system are not insane. We're not about to throw away all we've worked for and all we've accomplished because some slick lawyer says down is up and wrong is right—and finds a judge who agrees with him. We're going to find a way to put this matter to rest in a way that will satisfy us all.

Yes, we've got a job to do. And that is to get off that roller coaster, get control of our destiny and get on with the challenge of making Texaco the competitive leader in the world oil industry again. We don't come to work every day to be part of just a *good* company. We come to be part of a *great* company. If any of us expected less, we wouldn't be at Texaco. But there's more to winning than talent and desire. It takes a clear strategy and a solid plan to make sure that today's actions are driving toward tomorrow's gains.

> Some people may look at Texaco and see a lot of hardware… but when I look at Texaco, the first thing I see is the richness of our people and their potential.

Let's start by talking about what we mean by competition. Because that is the measure of everything we do. If there is one thing I think I really understand—perhaps stemming from my own early days in the Sales Department—it is competition.

I know that to be winners we must perform every job we do, not only as well as it can be done by our competitors, but so much better that they start to emulate us. But let's never underestimate our competitors. They are tough, aggressive, and they'll eat our lunch if we turn away from the table. And we have to be ready to repay the compliment.

We live in a world today that becomes more and more competitive as our economy matures. Performance that might have made a winner 25 years ago—or 10—won't make the cut today. As recently as 1972, Mark Spitz set seven world swimming records in the Olympics. Today, those times wouldn't even get him on the team.

The pace of competition in the business world has changed just as dramatically. We must keep up with, and even surpass, the faster pace of competition today. And we must do it not only with our price signs on the corner—that's the easy part—but at every step along the way. In our marketing, our refining, our distribution, our production, our exploration, and our support services—all as a low-cost, high-quality producer.

We also have to compete for public approval, for hearts and minds. Why? Because we are a publicly held company, owned by hundreds of thousands of shareholders who are watching to see if we are worthy of their trust. And because millions of Americans depend on the energy we deliver.

So everything we do is subject to public scrutiny. We're graded day in and day out. Now, I don't believe everything I read on that score—especially in the unlikely event that it's flattering. But a recent issue of *Forbes* provides occasion for some sobering reflection.

In their section ranking the international petroleum industry, Texaco appears last or next to last in each category measured— return on assets, growth in sales, growth in earnings. It's enough to ruin your afternoon—if you let it. But you see there's a bright side, too—from the bottom of the barrel, the only way to go is up.

Even with all that, can I still be proud of Texaco? You bet I can. I'm proud of its people, the assets we've built, and our reputation for honesty and integrity. But I'm not proud of our overall results—and I know you're not either.

And do I have a vision of the future? You bet I do. I see Texaco becoming one of the most admired companies not just in our industry—but in the world.

And I'm not pulling that out of thin air. I have a basis for my optimistic assessment of our prospects. It comes from another annual ranking of most admired companies, this one done by *Fortune* magazine. You see, *Fortune* has its own set of criteria for establishing these rankings. They include:

1. Quality of products and services.
2. Financial soundness.
3. Long-term investment value.
4. Quality of management.
5. Innovation.
6. Use of corporate assets.
7. Ability to attract, keep and develop talented people.
8. Community and environmental responsibility.

Now compare *Fortune*'s ideas about what makes a company admirable to these concepts:

1. "Products of proven high quality."
2. "Financially sound."
3. "Fair return to shareholders."
4. "Inspired leadership."
5. "Encourage... suggestions from employees."
6. "Maintain a record of productivity and profits."
7. "Provide opportunities for employees to... advance."
8. "Be a good corporate citizen."

Do any of those sound familiar to you? They should. All those phrases are from Texaco's own guiding principles—which appear framed in our offices and on company bulletin boards. And they are remarkably similar to *Fortune*'s criteria for what makes a company admirable.

These principles aren't just meant to be framed. They're meant to be lived. They belong in our vision and in our character.

Because you see, we already have a roadmap in place. And those principles are it. The challenge is to believe it, work on it and adapt it as the competitive situation changes—and follow it until we've reached our goal of being one of America's most admired companies.

Some changes will be required. But let's not be fearful of those changes. Our challenge is to manage that transition—to create positive change—and not let the pressure of change manage us.

Here's what we must do to meet that challenge:

First, we're going to set objectives for ourselves and for our operations. But let's not just set objectives for the sake of having something to point to at the end of the year to justify our existence. When we achieve our objectives, we must be able to demonstrate how we have really served the interests and built the strengths of this company.

We should not be afraid to set these goals high and to seek new approaches. We have to get "can't" out of our vocabulary—and purge the phrase "we've never done it that way."

Too many people think that if there were a better way to do things, we'd already be doing it. That's why the founder of Federal Express said he avoided people with impressive resumes—because that only means they have learned all the reasons why you can't do something new.

Bobby Kennedy, paraphrasing George Bernard Shaw, once said "Some men see things as they are and ask 'why?'; I see things as they never were and ask 'why not?'" Which of those questions have we been asking ourselves?

Second, we must make plans and stick to them. A plan that produces nothing more than an elegant explanation of why it was not achieved is a failure.

Third, we must improve the return on the assets with which we have been entrusted. And when I say return on assets, I include the book return as well as the cash return. Both are vital to the health of the company.

A better return on assets will provide growth for our shareholders, and this is important, because we have a great responsibility to our shareholders. We want to pay the best return we can to them for the use of their capital.

Our shareholders give us more than money. They give us their confidence. Our shareholders worked long and hard to earn their money. We have to work even harder to merit their trust in us.

But also important, a better return on assets will also provide growth and opportunity for all of us at Texaco today, and all those who will follow us in the future. We're all shareholders in Texaco—or have the opportunity to be. But we're more than that: we're people who have invested our talents and dedication and our working lives in Texaco.

> **Our shareholders give us more than money. They give us their confidence.**

When you come right down to it, Texaco is ours to build. So that means we all ought to think like owners, not passive trustees. We shouldn't make the mistake of thinking we're just hired hands brought in to run somebody else's company. Because if we do that, we're likely to fall prey to the rented car syndrome. When was the last time you washed a rented car?

If we think of this company as *our* car, we'll develop a sense of urgency about making things right—a sense of urgency about making the company better, stronger and more profitable. And we'll discover that the better things are for Texaco, the better they will be for each of us.

Finally, we must make more efficient use of human resources and talents, and by this I'm not hinting at never-ending personnel reductions. What I am suggesting is that every job be necessary, interesting and creative, and that every job contribute to our progress.

All of these ideas involve accountability. Accountability means being responsible for one's actions and recommendations. Accountability means standing behind the new projects we recommend.

Accountability means standing on substance, not just procedure. It means more than just making sure that all the right signatures are on a memo—it means making sure all the right ideas are in it.

Accountability means being more than the corporate equivalent of civil servants. We have to be professional entrepreneurs, ready to take some risks to add value for the corporation, instead of new layers of protection for ourselves.

Finally, accountability means getting away from wishful thinking in our analysis of new ventures. Although we may feel that our current investment is low, it is really very substantial. We remain in the investment business—to the tune of over $2 billion a year—and wise direction of this money can expand the company and secure the future.

> **Quality means meeting the customer's requirements in all respects.**

On the other side of the coin, failure can further deteriorate our balance sheet. Much of our operating earnings improvement over the past several years has come from getting rid of the losers and rectifying past mistakes. That's fine and I applaud the program.

But we don't have many losers left. If we do, let's root them out and go on to building the kind of company that can profitably supply six percent of the free world's oil. The kind of company in which employees take pride, and boast of being part of. The kind of company our stockholders are loyal to. And the kind of company people the world over can hold in esteem.

So what kind of people can succeed in the company I have just described?

The kind of people who take responsibility—and not just enjoy authority. Each of us should be conscious of the clear difference between the two.

The kind of people who truly put the company's interest before their own—confident that their own interest will be served by their dedication to the success of the enterprise.

The kind of people with brains and the common sense to use them. Again, there is an important distinction between those two ideas.

The kind of people with initiative, drive, a sense of urgency, a fire in the belly. I have always preferred a horse who needed a rein rather than a spur.

And the kind of people who share the vision that only perfect quality is good enough, and that second best is as good as last.

Speaking of quality, that's a word that in recent years has been widely used—and abused. And it has acquired some new meanings along the way. The one I like is that quality means meeting the customer's requirements in all respects.

But we must ask ourselves, "who is the customer?" The easy answer is "the motorist who drives up to our pumps." But that is not the only answer. In our business life, each of us has customers. Think about who yours really are. The stillman's customer, for example, is the downstream processing unit which demands on-spec, on-time feedstock. Another example is the crude trader, whose customer is the leaseholder who needs dependable, on-time pickups every time. *My* customers are you— the employees, the shareholders, and the Board of Directors.

Knowing our customers and meeting their requirements is a commitment to quality as the governing principle of our work, and the ultimate measure of our performance.

Adherence to this concept has become a fact of life for one of our major competitors—Japan. This commitment to quality has already dramatically improved the performance of our own chemical company and our Port Arthur Refinery. This is only the beginning.

Those of you who share these visions will find this an exciting place to work. There will be compensation based on real performance and promotion based on real merit. In our competitive world, we cannot do otherwise.

The ideas that I have developed in this talk are really pretty simple because our business is really pretty simple: cost, revenue, volume, expense. Each can be controlled—and each can lead to success.

It would be naive to think that success comes easily or that our goals can be reached without a tough journey over some rough roads. And I ask each of you to look at your responsibility, understand the problems you can solve, recognize where you can make a difference within Texaco—and get on with it. Do it now!

No one person can run a company. In our case, a company is 50,000 people committed to a common purpose. Each of whom has his own responsibility, and his own authority.

Am I proud of the people that make up Texaco? You bet I am. Do I have a vision of the future? You bet I do—and I want you to share it with me. The vision outlined today depends on each of us enthusiastically accepting our responsibility, and exercising our authority in the best way possible.

Because we can't let up until the day comes when we can pick up *Fortune* magazine and read that Texaco is one of the most admired companies in America.

That day is coming. The timetable is in our hands.

Bankruptcy

The "vision speech" certainly did not solve all our problems. But at least it opened the door and turned on the light. In a glowing article on February 22, 1987, *The New York Times* commented on the positive changes in the atmosphere and direction at Texaco. The *Times* article was upbeat about the possibilities for the future. But the article also raised the ominous possibility that only the threat of bankruptcy, or bankruptcy itself, would allow Texaco to solve its legal problems.* Unfortunately, the *Times* was right.

We had promised to appeal the outrageous jury verdict, but as things stood in Texas, we couldn't. Texas law required that before filing an appeal we had to post a bond in the amount of the judgment, and $10.5 billion literally exceeded the bonding capacity then available in the entire world. So we obtained a temporary restraining order from Federal District Court to block the bonding requirement; this order was sustained by the U.S. Second Circuit Court of Appeals.

But on Monday, April 6, 1987, the U.S. Supreme Court lifted that temporary restraining order. The Supreme Court in no way commented on the merits of the case; it held that state appeals must be exhausted before federal courts could take the case. The impact of this ruling was enormous: since we could not post the $10.5 billion bond, we faced the immediate danger of Pennzoil being allowed under Texas law to place liens on our assets throughout the United States—thereby forcing us into involuntary bankruptcy under the supervision of a court in Texas.

The week of April 6 was spent in face-to-face, serious, but fruitless negotiations with Pennzoil. Thus, the Texaco Board of Directors met on Saturday afternoon, April 11, to consider its options. There were really only three: submit to involuntary bankruptcy in Texas; pay Pennzoil their final demand of $5 billion; or elect protection under Chapter 11 of the federal bankruptcy laws.

Chapter 11 protects a corporation from its creditors while it produces a reorganization plan under the supervision of a federal judge. Thus it would forestall the bond requirement, and buy us time to pursue appellate and settlement options. But it is not a painless option:

---

* Bennett, Robert A., *"Winning Friends for Texaco When It Needs Them Most,"* The New York Times, *Sunday, Feb. 22, 1987, p. E2.*

dividends cannot be paid to shareholders, significant control of the company passes to the federal bankruptcy judge, and various interested parties are organized in committees that peer into the company's affairs in order to protect their piece of the pie.

It sounds like an agonizing decision, but it really wasn't; difficult and long though the road would be, Chapter 11 appeared to offer Texaco the only hope of a fair review of the case and a secure financial future for the company, its shareholders and its employees. The Board was ready to vote late Saturday evening, but took one more night to sleep on it.

At 11:20 a.m. on April 12, 1987, Palm Sunday, the Board of Directors voted to use Chapter 11. Texaco was the largest U.S. company ever to take such an action. Al DeCrane and I immediately left for New York City to explain to a worldwide newspaper and television audience what had been done and why it was necessary.

In a crowded auditorium we began explaining the situation, but in a matter of seconds the reporters all shouted for us to stop. The enormous number of cameras, lights and recorders had blown out the available power supply, and we had to start again.

Our key message was that all of the company's creditors and suppliers would be paid in full and with interest in accordance with applicable law—and that Chapter 11 protection was being sought because it represented the only way to make it possible for us to appeal this insane Texas judgment.

We used no prepared scripts at the news conference; the words transcribed from the videotape show that the occasion was pretty emotional for me: "I can truthfully tell you that this process has been enormously painful.... I love this company and I have devoted the last 32 years of my life to working for it.... We can answer to our shareholders and employees that today's action had to be taken to safeguard tomorrow's future."

Leaving the office that evening, I was still under a cloud. My wife had driven over in the morning to accompany me to New York, so we had two cars to drive home. I followed her out the drive, and suddenly she stopped and ran back to my car. I instantly thought, "what more can possibly happen to me today?" She said, "Guess what, the radio says Larry Mize won the Masters at Augusta by chipping in on the eleventh hole!" That made me laugh, and it felt good; Mary had given me a thoughtful reminder that Texaco's trouble was not the only thing on the news that day—and that no matter what the difficulty, life does go on.

There was a standing ovation from the employees on Monday morning as we walked into the Texaco auditorium to explain the events of the weekend. But then began the uncharted voyage of operating a major international oil company under the protection of Chapter 11.

Somebody asked me what Chapter 11 was like, and I replied that it was akin to undressing in Macy's window on the day before Christmas. As the days went by in kaleidoscopic succession after April, all of us at Texaco discovered the truth of that statement. The required bankruptcy committees were formed, made up of equity holders, creditors and competitors—and each of them, armed with dozens of lawyers, sought to further its own interests and to delve into every aspect of the company's business.

The following month, on May 12, the company's Annual Meeting was to be held in Denver. There we would have the opportunity to explain to a thousand concerned shareholders why they were, at least temporarily, receiving no dividends. Al DeCrane, Texaco's Board Chairman, delivered a clear and detailed account of the legal situation and an overview of current conditions in the oil business (which was a relief, in a way; sometimes it seemed hard to remember that we were still running an oil company!). Then I outlined our plans for the company's future.

MILEPOST: MAY 12, 1987

Address to 1987 Annual Meeting of Texaco Shareholders

Denver

I want to take a few moments to underscore some of the points about the case in Texas, because, frankly, we can't address the operations of our company without taking into account the effect this litigation has had on our business.

Like you, our shareholders, I wish that this discussion of the Pennzoil litigation—and the factors that led Texaco to seek protection under Chapter 11—were a *post mortem* to an unhappy event that had been concluded. I look forward to that day, and to meeting with you to report instead on substantial improvements in the company's performance.

To paraphrase Winston Churchill, we're not here to preside over the liquidation of this company. Texaco is a proud name that stands for integrity and quality in more than 150 countries around the world, and I'm convinced it will be a vital and thriving company in the future.

I certainly didn't intend to begin my tenure as Chief Executive Officer, or address my first Annual Meeting, under the cloud of Chapter 11. But then I never dreamed the law that we all trust and respect could be so distorted, or that our adversaries could be so blinded by greed as to become, in the end, irrational.

Filing for bankruptcy was a serious, painful, wrenching decision—one that will have significant effects on every operation of our company, on our employees, and on you, our stockholders. It certainly won't speed the process of meeting the urgent challenges facing our company and the rest of the petroleum industry.

In the end, there's one and only one reason we took the action we did: to protect the assets in which you have invested some of the proceeds from your life's work and to preserve the future of the company you helped build. We faced the decision of safeguarding all those assets—or seeing them picked off, one by one. In effect, through Pennzoil's intransigence, its extortionist efforts to dismember our company and the financial deterioration that resulted, the right decision became clear. If Pennzoil had been allowed to get in the driver's seat, your interests would have come in a distant last.

Fortunately, we were not alone as we faced this decision. In fact, Al and I can't say enough about the way your Board of Directors has conducted itself throughout this difficult period.

They have given of themselves—with their utmost concern and being—for your interests as shareholders. We want to take this moment to express to them our deep admiration and gratitude for their tireless efforts in dealing with the consequences of this gross miscarriage of justice.

And it would be a gross miscarriage of justice if Texaco cannot overcome what has befallen it as a result of Pennzoil's wildcatting in the Texas courts.

This issue has become more than a crisis for Texaco and for all of us as shareholders and employees. It has also suggested a lack of confidence in our legal system—and, in the eyes of many foreign observers, a question as to our nation's reliability as a place in which to invest and to do business.

To ensure that we can continue to protect your interests, we made the right decision at the right time. That decision, in fact, has bought us the ability to pursue a successful appeal or to negotiate a reasonable settlement, should that be possible. The important thing is to put this grim episode in Texaco's proud 85-year history behind us, so that we can put all our energies into strengthening the company's asset base and improving its return to shareholders.

In order to ensure that result, we have continued, despite the pressing demands of the litigation, to carry on the work of restoring Texaco to a leading competitive position in the international oil industry.

So let's now turn to the real business of a company that supplies six percent of the free world's oil. We're trying to regain competitive leadership at a tough juncture.

Not only have we had Pennzoil breathing down our necks—it also isn't exactly the best of times out in the oil patch.

Two weeks ago Texaco reported its earnings for the first quarter of 1987. It was a quarter characterized by a slight improvement in crude prices compared to the end of 1986, but still substantially lower than the level of the first quarter last year.

Crude prices had moved downward erratically since the first quarter of 1986, while the producing nations produced more oil for the market than it could absorb.

The oversupply of both crude oil and refined products has depressed not only the profitability of Texaco's worldwide equity crude production, but also price and margins in our refining and marketing businesses.

Earnings for the first quarter were $118 million, or 49 cents a share. This level is not satisfactory to us, but I believe that with continued expense control and some improvement in price and margins, better results should be forthcoming, and we are determined to achieve a more competitive return on assets. We have a sound strategy in place to accomplish that, and we're already moving forward on the right course.

> **Those who remain can be confident that the work they do is essential.... In the long run, everyone will win.**

Each business segment has been analyzed to determine whether it is helping us gain an edge on the competition. We will continue to build on those that are strong. Those assets which cannot measure up have been, or are being, eliminated.

Our commitment to competitive leadership extends not only to operations but to our administrative and support organizations as well.

We are currently completing a thorough analysis of jobs in the company. This analysis is tough-minded and realistic. Each job must prove itself to be necessary and productive.

We could have eliminated jobs across the board, and by fiat from the top. Instead we chose a more thorough, thoughtful approach—an analysis to measure each job's contribution to the bottom line. And we invited employees throughout the company to be part of this process.

Those who remain can be confident that the work they do is essential to the success and future of the company. In the long run, everyone will win.

The company recently completed a major, five-year refinery modernization program. This program gave us an edge in the important motor gasoline market. There is a growing demand for cleaner, lighter, more valuable products, and we are positioned to meet that demand.

Our investments in marketing will allow us not only to meet the competition but to beat it. Texaco is leading the industry in the direction of high-volume, high-profit stations on good real estate. Our System 2000 outlets have been consistent winners in the U.S. and Europe.

The exploration and producing side of our business has also been enhanced by the long-term investment programs of recent years.

In the first half of this decade, Texaco rebuilt its worldwide acreage position. That effort has continued, as evidenced by our recent acquisition of 34 tracts in the April Gulf of Mexico sale.

Exploration programs in general have long lead times and delayed recognition of success. Nevertheless, the bottom line on an exploration and production program is the reserves ultimately booked.

I hope you have noticed that in the past two years, Texaco's reserve reports have shown positive upward revisions, adding reserves on top of the increases brought about by current new discoveries.

Throughout the world, we have set the standard for low lifting cost operations.

One day the world will need all the oil that can be economically produced.* We'll be there with enough crude to provide a steady supply of products to consumers—but only in a way that also provides a secure stream of earnings for our shareholders.

During this period of reorganization under Chapter 11 we are also continuing our planning to make the company's securities more attractive to their owners.

As we emerge from reorganization, our plan is to:

▓ Improve the profitability of each asset.
▓ Optimize the cash flow available for reinvestment.
▓ And maximize our shareholders' return through dividends and higher stock values.

These, then, are some of the plans and goals we have set for our company. These goals are clear—only the timetable is uncertain. But we are committed to making it happen as soon as possible.

---

* *For years, predictions have been made that either, (1) the world is running out of oil, or (2) a substitute for fossil fuel is right on the horizon; by end of the year 2001, neither had come to pass. From 1985 to 1998, U.S. oil consumption increased from 15.94 to 18.92 million barrels per day and world consumption from 59.77 to 73.85 million barrels per day.*

The situation we find ourselves in today proves the poet Bobby Burns' observation about the best-laid plans of mice and men. But this situation also proves that just as important as the right *plans* is the right *attitude*.

For example, in the four months since we undertook our new responsibilities, Al and I have traveled to many Texaco operations worldwide. We have met or talked to nearly 20,000 employees and worked not just to explain our plans, but also to instill the attitudes that will bring those plans to fruition.

We've told them what I've told you today—how we plan to put Texaco's assets and people to their most efficient and most productive use.

But we've also told them that for those plans to produce success, we need their help and support. We've challenged them to reach for top levels of competitive performance every day:

We've asked our Texaco people:

- To think like owners, not simply hired managers.
- To use their imagination.
- To stretch their minds and their talents.
- To write that unwritten memo that will tell us how to produce the highest revenue at the lowest cost, increase the cash flow available for reinvestment and our shareholders, and increase the book earnings from which dividends will be declared.

And we've made it clear that we're looking for the kind of people who are willing to accept accountability. By accountability, I mean:

- Taking responsibility, not just enjoying authority—standing on substance, not procedure.
- Adding value for stockholders—not new layers of protection for ourselves.
- Showing initiative, drive, a sense of urgency.

In return, what we can offer is an exciting environment for those who share our vision—and rewards for those who take risks that produce results.

The response has been tremendous.

This is a company of many parts, but as times get tough, it is working with one heart, one mind, and one goal. Our people make this company work. They are more than equal to the challenge facing us. They are determined to keep the Texaco star the proud symbol of achievement it has always been.

With their help and support, I believe we can continue to make progress during these difficult days.

And when we do, you who have stood with us in these darkest days, who agonized with us as we agonized, struggled with us as we struggled, invested your savings as we invested our very beings in your company—your celebration and your share in our success will be the greatest of all.

Another setback in court

At the conclusion of this address to the 1987 Annual Meeting, the audience broke into a standing ovation—not quite a unanimous one, but very supportive nonetheless.

One shareholder asked, "You have said this morning that Texaco has done no wrong. So why did you offer Pennzoil $2 billion to settle? Why do they deserve a bloody cent?" The question was greeted with a round of applause—as was my reply: "In all seriousness, I ask myself the same question!" But then I offered an answer in down-home terms, "The ox is in the ditch, and this management is going to get him out."

But not yet. Because what the immediate future held was more bad news. Our appeal of the Texas trial court's decision made its way to the Supreme Court of Texas, made up of nine judges who were elected in statewide elections financed largely by the plaintiff's bar.

The Attorneys General of 20 states had submitted *amicus curiae* briefs urging the Texas high court to review the decision. The Chairman of the federal Securities and Exchange Committee submitted a brief pointing out that SEC Rule 10b-13 (prohibiting purchases of stock, or contracts to purchase stock, during a tender offer) had been violated—and thus, no legal contract could have existed for Pennzoil's purchase of an interest in Getty. Four former U.S. Secretaries of the Treasury had also submitted an *amicus curiae* brief on Texaco's side.

Despite these fervent pleas from thoughtful officials in the rest of the U.S., on November 2, 1987 the Texas Supreme Court ruled that it would not review the case as "no reversible error" existed—and that, unbelievably, the case was not even worthy of a hearing. Once again we had to go to the public and explain the inexplicable. My remarks were presented in a paper that was carefully prepared by counsel and released to the press after the Court made its appalling ruling. We had hesitated to make such strong statements before, while the state of Texas had jurisdiction— but now there was no longer any reason not to "tell it like it is!"

MILEPOST: NOVEMBER 3, 1987

An 'Incomprehensible' Decision in Texas Supreme Court

White Plains, New York

Yesterday's court decision is incomprehensible. We had expected to hear that the Supreme Court of Texas had decided to take full advantage of its opportunity to dispel the cloud of controversy hanging over the Texaco-Pennzoil litigation.

Instead, we learned of a much different decision—a decision that defied logic and law. The Texas Supreme Court's decision not to review the Texaco-Pennzoil litigation disregards justice and glosses over the many grave questions of respect for law, due process and elementary principles of judicial conduct arising out of this case.

We will promptly file an appeal with the United States Supreme Court that will focus on many of these questions, including:

- Whether a company can enjoy a massive benefit from an alleged contract pursued in direct violation of the federal securities laws, as found by the agency charged with enforcing those laws.
- Whether a fair trial was possible when the chief lawyer for one side in a case had contributed and raised large sums of money for the trial judge after the case began. And whether the trial judge's refusal to step aside, asserting that "mere bias or prejudice" is no ground for a judge to be disqualified, is consistent with our notions of justice and what a judge is supposed to be.
- Whether the applicable laws of sister states regarding contracts, business competition, damages and fiduciary duty will be faithfully and consistently applied, as the U.S. Constitution requires.

Inexplicably, the Texas Supreme Court has turned a deaf ear to those who have raised serious questions concerning these issues—the United States Securities and Exchange Commission, and the states of New York and Delaware, the very jurisdictions whose laws govern this case. And it has ignored the considered opinions and legal briefs not just of these experts, but of other states, labor unions, business leaders, legal scholars, economists and many others around the nation.

This is a case in which the U.S. Securities and Exchange Commission has taken the extraordinary step of intervening to say, with no equivocation, that Pennzoil "plainly violated" federal securities laws by trying to make a private contract to buy Getty while its public tender offer was still outstanding. The Texas Courts have now made it quite clear that they do not intend to give effect to the federal securities laws.

We expect the Texas Court's disregard for Federal law, as expressed by the SEC, to be taken very seriously by the U.S. Supreme Court. Over the last 10 years, the SEC's position has been sustained on the merits by the High Court in all seven of the cases in which it has intervened in behalf of the petitioner as a friend of the court.

And we do not expect that the Texas Courts' conclusion that "mere bias or prejudice" does not disqualify a trial judge under the Texas law is going to pass muster under the due process clause of the United States Constitution as the U.S. Supreme Court sees it.

This is the 200th anniversary of the U.S. Constitution. The Texas Supreme Court had a model case—a chance to show the nation how one state could treat the laws of a sister state with respect and care in judicial proceedings, and how a state's top court could insist that the state's lower courts must provide the fairness and constitutional due process to any American citizen, individual or corporate, no matter what state they're from. It didn't happen.

Some 18 states in addition to New York and Delaware have appeared in this case to register their concern about the lack of respect shown by the Texas courts for the laws of New York and Delaware. Yesterday's action flaunts this unequivocal call for a review of this case.

As disappointing as yesterday's development is, Texaco is prepared to move forward. We are confident that with the many federal statutory and constitutional issues raised during the course of this litigation, we will receive a full hearing and fair treatment in the nation's highest court.

While we continue, as we have in the past, to remain open to a reasonable and economic resolution of this case, we will not allow this unjust and ill-considered decision to be the basis for an extortionate settlement that would severely damage the interests of hundreds of thousands of Texaco shareholders, employees and business partners.

Texaco's business will continue in its normal course as we take steps to continue our legal case. Under the provisions of Chapter 11 of the U.S. bankruptcy code, Pennzoil will not be permitted to encumber our assets or to interfere with our business relationships. We will continue to meet our financial obligations to our creditors on a current basis, to market our products to our customers throughout the world, and to ensure continue payment of benefits to our retirees.

My greatest regret about Chapter 11 is the hardship it has caused for Texaco's stockholders. Many of them have relied for years on the company's unbroken record of dividend payments. Yet there has been a tremendous outpouring of support from our stockholders. They recognize that the unreasonable demands placed on our company by Pennzoil in the course of this litigation have made Chapter 11 protection necessary to preserve this company's assets for them—always our first and foremost objective.

We have been greatly encouraged by stockholders who have told us to hang in there and fight this injustice.

The stockholders committee in the Chapter 11 proceedings who independently reviewed this case concluded that Pennzoil's claim was totally without merit. They went to the extraordinary effort of submitting a brief to the Texas Supreme Court telling the court of their conclusions.

Additionally, I want to emphasize that the company's success in coping with a difficult situation is the result of the energy, hard work and talents of our employees. Their dedication and support is deeply appreciated.

We will fulfill our responsibility to our Texaco people and preserve this great company for generations to come by availing ourselves of the full protection of our nation's highest law, the Constitution.

And we fully expect to win this appeal to the Supreme Court. The laws support us. Those jurisdictions that wrote the laws support us. And simple fairness and justice support us.

The settlement

The Texas Supreme Court's inaction came as other developments were unfolding that would have an impact on Texaco.

Over the previous months, an Australian investor, Robert Holmes à Court, had acquired about 12 percent of Texaco's shares on the open market. He had done so largely with borrowed money. Bankruptcy forced Texaco to suspend its dividend in April 1987, and then the U.S. stock market dropped 25 percent in a single day, October 25, 1987. This investor, who had been quite supportive of Texaco management, suddenly had a very real cash-flow problem. His solution was to sell his shares, and in November he did so, at about $38 per share. They were purchased by American speculator Carl Icahn.

Icahn is no passive shareholder, as will be seen in the next chapter. He immediately insinuated himself into the Company's then ongoing negotiations with Pennzoil to settle the suit. His ideas of settlement, however, were at a considerably higher price than management wanted (and eventually achieved).

Although the best legal advice we had was that the U.S. Supreme Court *would* probably reverse the Texas decision if it accepted the case for review, it was not certain that the Supreme Court would accept it. Most Americans think they have a sure right to have the U.S. Supreme Court hear their appeal, but there is no such automatic right. The Court takes only those relatively few cases it believes have potential importance as precedents.

This uncertainty was making it increasingly difficult to handle the financial demands of a major worldwide enterprise. With the prodding of the Federal Bankruptcy Court applied to both sides (with perhaps more practicality than idealism), the case was settled during the wee hours of Saturday morning, December 19. The price was steep: $3 billion.

On Monday morning, December 21, 1987, we walked into the company's auditorium to explain the settlement to Texaco employees. This time there was no standing ovation. The decision to settle had been driven by necessity—but by that decision, our opportunity to appeal to the highest court in the land had been foregone. This was a bitter pill for every employee, including the CEO, to swallow.

Sometimes a news photo can capture the feeling of the moment better than any written words. On Sunday morning, *The New York*

Times had sent to our house a photographer, Suzanne DeChillo, who had been assigned to photograph the opposing CEOs in the case. She was a very sympathetic person who started out by promising, "We'll make you look like someone out of *Chariots of Fire*, and make him look like Tom Jones!" She did one formal shot and then, seeing my wife and myself in an unguarded moment, asked if she could do a candid picture outside.

That picture, taken in dense fog by a bare apple tree, with two very pensive people and two apparently very understanding dogs, told the story.

2

The Takeover Fight

We now concentrated on the next phase of the battle. We needed a plan for reorganization that would enable us to escape from Chapter 11—and then to create a new, smaller Texaco able to compete around the world and serve its shareholders and its customers, while providing a future for its employees. This had to be done in the face of a determined effort to take over the company, by a speculator with a very different agenda.

Our plan for the "new" Texaco was submitted to Bankruptcy Court; it proposed the sale of many properties, including our German affiliate, about one-half of our U.S. refining and marketing system, and eventually our Canadian affiliate.

Carl Icahn had submitted his own plan for our reorganization to the Court, with some added twists of his own. He would have had the court eliminate the company's corporate governance provisions for such things as staggered terms on the Board, a shareholder rights plan and a fair price provision—the absence of which would have made it easier for him to seize control of Texaco at a bargain price. The bankruptcy judge did not agree with him, and it was our reorganization plan, not Icahn's, that was approved.

On April 7, 1988, having satisfied all its creditors, Texaco was released from the supervision of the Bankruptcy Court—and from the numerous intrusive committees, their lawyers and their investment advisers that were all a part of the bankruptcy proceedings. It would have been nice to have felt more relief than we did; as things stood, the decision simply cleared the decks for the battle with Icahn.

Icahn reiterated his interest in taking over the company, and continued buying shares—gradually increasing his stake from 12 percent to 18 percent.

While Texaco and Icahn both professed dedication to the shareholders, each had quite different views of the company's future. This situation made a proxy fight inevitable. Icahn filed to elect his own slate of directors. Both sides enriched the newspapers as they fired salvos of full-page ads finding fault with the veracity, the intentions, and generally the lineage of the other.

The company's plans were to sell assets, re-deploy the capital, and re-create one of the world's leading petroleum companies. Mr. Icahn's plans were less defined, but included buying the company, dividing it up and selling the parts, thus realizing a large short-term gain.

Every campaign must have a theme. Texaco's was: "We do what we say we are going to do." Each message began with that, and followed with a description of our plans. This message was brought to every shareholder who wanted to hear it—by phone, press, and a traveling team of six executives who talked to shareholder groups in 18 cities in 21 days. The format for this "fight team" presentation was simple and effective: refreshments, roast beef sandwiches, a short speech, and questions and answers.

The individual shareholders were largely sympathetic and supportive. Institutional investors, however, were believed to be less so.

The Council of Institutional Investors, which represented many large public-sector pension funds, arranged for Icahn and me to appear before them. Nell Minow, reporting on the CII meeting, subsequently wrote:

> "Both Kinnear and Icahn appeared before a special meeting of the Council of Institutional Investors to state their cases. The sentiments of those in the room were geared slightly toward Icahn when Kinnear appeared to make the first presentation... First, he said that he had every penny of his own money in Texaco. There is no better guarantee of scrupulous attention to shareholder value than a CEO whose net worth depends on it, and this had an enormous impact. He talked about the oil business and his plans for the future once the

bankruptcy was behind them. Everyone in the room could feel his commitment, his enthusiasm, his expertise. Icahn came in. He did not give any specifics about his plans for the company, and he could not claim that he put everything he had into Texaco. The group was open-minded, but he just could not compete."*

It would be personally gratifying to report that all large state pension funds and institutions voted for management. They did not. However, the percentage of those who did vote for the continued existence of the company was higher than in most contests of this kind, and that made a real difference.

An unusually high percentage of the stock in Texaco—about 12 percent—was held by company employees. The employees themselves were determined that the takeover attempt would not be successful. After the problems of the previous years, they fervently wanted the opportunity to put their lives back together and continue their employment with a successful, well-thought-of international oil company. In one sense there was of course an element of self-preservation. But in a much larger sense there was a proud, fierce personal determination to win one for the shareholders.

The themes of honesty, integrity and dedication to shareholder value were played literally around the world—but still the contest was in doubt. As the management team assembled at Tulsa for the Annual Meeting to be held on June 17, our people were still working the phones. Several large shareholders called in with their intention to support management; others called and changed their votes the other way.

Despite all the preliminary canvassing, as we assembled in the ballroom of the Westin Hotel, there were 60 million shares represented by proxies in the room yet to be voted. The scene would have done justice to a Hollywood movie: the opposition in uniformly dark pinstripes and I in a light blue Glen plaid suit for contrast; the mayor of Tulsa wearing a red star badge reading "Tulsa Loves Texaco"; company employees dressed in red dresses at each microphone; reporters, photographers, ballot boxes and loudspeakers. The company's future was on the line.

---

* *Monks, Robert G., and Nell Minow,* Power and Accountability, *Harper Business, New York, 1991, p. 37.*

MILEPOST: JUNE 17, 1988

Address to Shareholders on the Proxy Fight with Carl Icahn

Texaco Annual Meeting, Tulsa, Oklahoma

———

As we address the issue of Texaco's future, I am reminded of a remark by Mark Twain that concisely summarizes the philosophy that has brought us so far. He once opined, "Always do right. This will gratify some people, and it will astonish the rest."

And that is the real issue here today: choosing the right people and the right plan to lead Texaco into the future, to lead this company and to carry out our restructuring plan.

Texaco has nominated, in addition to your Chief Executive Officer, four dedicated and experienced members of your outstanding current Board of Directors. I'm Jim Kinnear and I was a trainee in a service station in Chicago 34 years ago, and I worked in every operating department in this company.*

We believe that we have put together the right plan for restoring Texaco to competitive leadership. Our plan is big. Our plan is real and our plan is now. It is based on the building of value both today and for the future. And what is most exciting is the extent to which we have already begun to put it in place and to do exactly what we said we were going to do.

As we said we would, we've emerged from Chapter 11 with a plan that repaid all of our creditors, resolved other major contingent liabilities, and yet provided the flexibility that we needed to move forward.

As we said we would, we acted within days of our emergence from Chapter 11 to reinstate the regular 75 cents quarterly dividend.

---

* *Hands-on experience in marketing, refining, and producing operations proved to be an invaluable asset in a time of crisis, because operating decisions could be made quickly without laborious background analysis.*

And as we said we would, we have increased your company's profitability and made excellent progress in a major restructuring designed to provide a prompt and substantial enhancement in the value of your shares.

Just yesterday we signed a detailed letter of intent with Aramco Services Company, representing the government of Saudi Arabia, to form a joint venture for refining and market-ing petroleum products on the east and Gulf coasts of the United States. We expect to achieve approximately $2 billion in direct cash benefits and savings from this partnership.

So it fits right into the financial criteria that we set for our own joint venture efforts under our restructur-ing plan.

Just as important, this joint venture ties into another aspect of Texaco's restructur-ing—our determination to reorganize and strengthen our ongoing operations to gener-ate additional substantial growth over the near term and over the long term.

Our plan is big. Our plan is real and our plan is now.

We have announced the sale of a Texaco subsidiary for over $1.2 billion. The value of this restructuring step is to obtain that cash for other use and the elimination of the downstream from Germany.

We are receiving bids today for a number of marginal produc-ing properties in this country. These sales will eliminate over-head, will improve book earnings and will generate cash that can be better put into other investments.

In a very important step, we have announced that we intend to distribute directly to you, the shareholders, more than $1.7 billion from the $5 billion-plus proceeds of those and other expected asset sales, through a stock buy-back or other distribu-tion program for completion before the end of the year. Equally important, the balance of that $5 billion owned by you, the shareholders, will be there creating value for you by paying down debt and by further improving the asset base.

All these actions demonstrate your Board's and management's commitment, and its ability to bring about a prompt enhance-ment of shareholder value while building a stronger and a more productive company.

More positive actions will follow. We will move forward with additional restructuring steps based on these criteria to identify and to sell the less productive assets—ones that will be worth more to someone else than they might be to us—and to expand our most productive areas while reducing debt to competitive levels. This plan will maximize earnings per year, and cash-flow per share. They will optimize the financial ratios and maximize the dividend coverage.

I have been asked often about the Icahn Group's proposal—which we believe presents a stark and a negative contrast. To this philosophy of ours—one of building values for all share-holders—contrast that put forward by the Icahn Group.

Initially Texaco was besieged by a variety of proposals by the Icahn Group, all designed to allow the sale of a significant por-tion of their stock back to the company on terms that we believe were unduly preferential to them and not in keeping with our commitment to fairness and to value for all shareholders.

Therefore, we rejected the group's demands. We made that decision despite frequent reminders that if we couldn't agree, there would be a proxy contest and a bear-hug proposal. So that's what we have today.

The Icahn Group still has no financing, no partners of substance and no explanation for its $6 billion in errors and discrepancies.

I've been asked why that bear hug hasn't been sent out to the shareholders for a sepa-rate specific vote at some future specific shareholders' meetings. It hasn't because that proposal wasn't and isn't real. It has no financ-ing plan. In the opinion of Morgan Stanley, it could not be financed. The more we have learned about that plan, and Mr. Icahn's state-ments about it, the more strongly that analysis has held up—because despite constant contact with a wide number of banks and potential partners, the Icahn Group still has no financing, no partners of substance and no explanation for its $6 billion in errors and discrepancies. In short, no real offer.

The approach from the Icahn Group really amounts to the proposition that they be designated as the broker for the breakup and the sale of this company's assets—*your* assets.

If there is any doubt with regard to the intentions of the Icahn Group, we shareholders need no further evidence than the speed with which they announced their intent to sell Caltex, a most profitable component of any long-term plan for the suc-cessful future of Texaco.

We don't need months of delay for special meetings, thou-sands of additional letters and millions of additional phone calls to you and to others to decide whether the shareholders want to restructure or destructure, restructure or destroy this company. That issue is before us in the form of the slate that you elect.

As you know, the shareholders have a right to place proposals before the shareholders at any annual meeting. The Icahn Group could have placed its so-called offer before you at this meeting. They did not. They have asked you to call a special meeting during the months ahead. The uncertainty would interfere with our ability to complete our restructuring that is already going so well. To delay and perhaps to lose the benefits of our restructuring—to argue one more time the merits of this illusory offer—would not, we believe, serve the interests of shareholders.

As has been publicly reported, we do intend to meet with representatives of our large public fund shareholders to discuss the nomination by the Board of individuals identified by the public funds to be voted upon in the election of directors at the 1989 Annual Meeting. We believe that such funds can help us to continue to obtain outstanding individuals to serve on our Board, which will benefit all shareholders.

Public institutional investors play an increasingly important role in owning the shares of Texaco, and they hold an important interest in Texaco's long-term health and success. Your Board believes that this role can benefit all shareholders.

Today we face a critical choice as to the future of one of the world's great companies. The choice is between action that is already under way, to build value for you—or an illusory plan whose ultimate aim is to dismantle Texaco. In the interest not only of a productive company—a productive economy, energy security and fiduciary responsibility—but also your own financial security, the Texaco slate is the most responsible choice.

During the last several weeks I have traveled to 14 cities, across the length and breadth of this country, to meet with many of you. You made it clear to us that promises, programs and pep talks are great. But you want results.

Let me say to you today that we have heard you, loud and clear. We have made an excellent start toward meeting your concerns and building the value of your shares. We will be distributing major portions of that value to you in the weeks and months to come, and we are going to do more.

We thank you again for the support that you have shown us so far, and we commit to you that with your continued support we are going to build a new and a stronger and a more productive

Texaco for all of its shareholders. A company of which all of us—
employees and shareholders alike—can be proud.

We have told ourselves that we intend to make this company
one of the most admired companies in the United States, and we
mean it. Our Board means it, and I mean it. Thank you very much.

■

Back to work

Very quickly after the meeting, the Corporation Trust Company calculated a vote favoring management of 56 percent to 44 percent.

"Did you win? Did you win?" some weary employees were asked as they entered an elevator after the meeting. The employees just grinned. It was really the shareholders who won. For the period from December 31, 1985 through August 31, 1999, Texaco shareholders received a total return of 825.2 percent, for a compound growth rate of 17.7 percent per year—while Pennzoil shareholders suffered a decline of 17.4 percent in their investment, a loss of 1.4 percent per year.*

These results, from the period after the judgment until the time Pennzoil disappeared as an independent company, suggest that a windfall is not always a blessing, and that adversity can truly be made the father of success.

The adversity we had suffered spurred us to prove to the shareholders that they had made the right decision—and pushed us to motivate the company in a new direction. After three years of corporate warfare there was a need to set new objectives to improve the company's competitive position. The company was now considerably smaller, having left about one-third of its equity in District Court 151 of Houston, Texas; we were going to have to run even harder to compete in the demanding arena of international petroleum. Projects were established in each functional area and in each staff department to replace the exigencies of battle with equally important targets in the oil patch.

For a while Carl Icahn remained Texaco's largest shareholder, owning over 18 percent of the Company's outstanding common stock. Cordial relations with him were established. In January 1989 the company announced a special dividend and a stock buy-back program to the benefit of all shareholders. On June 2, 1989 Mr. Icahn sold his 43,000,000 shares into a rising market. Peace had broken out.

---

* *These figures were calculated by the Research Department of PaineWebber Incorporated, and contained in a letter dated September 9, 1999.*

3

Leadership in Crisis

In the heat of the Pennzoil-Icahn crises, all of the senior officers of Texaco were much too preoccupied with the job at hand to spend time reflecting on the lessons we were learning along the way. But after the crisis was over we found ourselves being described as having provided the "crisis leadership" that was critical to the company's survival. That, in turn, forced us to reflect more on just what we had accomplished—and how. What does it take to provide "leadership"?

Describing leadership, or reciting the qualities that distinguish a leader, is somewhat akin to taking a tape measure to a jellyfish. Leaders have different styles, different objectives, and different personality traits.

Some leaders are outstanding orators who can rouse an audience. Others lead by personal example—or by obvious intellectual brilliance. Some are aloof, introspective characters who issue directives from on high; others are approachable, first-name types, who form strong personal bonds. Some are almost self-effacing; some glory in the recital of their own importance.

If we think of leaders we have known, or known about, we can surely put some names to each of these categories. Each became a successful leader by making the most of whatever skills he or she possessed, and whatever forces or assets were available to be deployed. Julius Caesar,

Martin Luther King, Jr., and Casey Stengel were three very different men with very different approaches—but each was a successful leader.

It is too easy to think that leaders are born and not made. Of course some elements of personality and physique are genetic in nature. But training and environment can play a large role in the development of successful leadership. And yes, in that sense leadership can be taught. Not every student of it will go down in history, but each can be improved, and each can learn to use the abilities and resources at hand in a more effective way.

Perhaps the first step in learning how to be a leader is learning how to follow one. Some very wise leaders have helped me along the way in my career, although sometimes the assistance came in a package that was not instantly recognizable. One lesson I didn't appreciate fully at the time had to do with followership.

In the summer of 1953, at the end of the Korean War, I received orders to proceed from Korea, where I had spent three tours of duty in the combat area, to take up an assignment as aide to the Commandant of the Ninth Naval District, Rear Admiral Francis P. Old. Now in the Navy, an admiral's aide—while not thought of as an archangel—is certainly ranked right up there with the cherubim. I was resplendent with bright new gold aiguillettes and three rows of service ribbons from Korea, and was obviously more than a little proud of myself.

On Monday morning, my first day on the job, the Admiral called me to his office, sat me down and offered some advice: "Jimmy, let me tell you one thing: In this office, I wear the stars, and you don't!"

At the moment I wasn't totally sure what he was driving at, but on sober reflection I decided to be a little more humble, and keep one pace to the left and one pace behind my admiral. We became great friends, and I truly believe that his stern words were carefully thought out to forestall trouble. And his advice is still valuable—especially to those who consider themselves on the fast track.

Leadership by example is generally a lot more effective than "Do as I say, not as I do."

But leadership by example was simpler when the world was simpler. You can find an example in Book IV of Caesar's *Commentaries on the Gallic Wars*. Julius Caesar put the first bridge over the Rhine, and in his writings he described in great detail how the bridge was built on piles driven into the river bottom at a slant, to resist the current.

Caesar obviously knew everything there was to know in the 1st Century B.C. about how to build a bridge.* In today's increasingly technical environment it is an unusual leader who can personally know every detail of the operation he must lead. But technical unfamiliarity is no excuse. It is up to the leader to learn at least the whys and wherefores, and certainly to be familiar with the vocabulary of the operation. Most forms of endeavor have their own vocabularies, and managers of these activities seem to delight in "snowing" the boss with their specialized command of the details. The boss, on the other hand, has the responsibility to know enough about the operation to be able to ask the right questions.

There's an old saying: "The boss needs to know where the broom is." In an oil company the boss may not have to be able to design a crude still, but he or she should surely know how one operates. Beyond that, good leaders must surround themselves with associates who are skilled in the areas with which the leader is least familiar—and good leaders are not afraid to consult these associates.

I had a chance to reflect on crisis leadership when invited to speak to the Young Presidents Organization about Texaco's path through its crisis. The Young Presidents Organization is an association of some of the outstanding business leaders in the United States. To be a member, before reaching the age of 40 one must have become the president of an independent company that does at least $10 million a year in sales. It is an active organization; the members learn from each other as they trade stories of successes (and, less often, failures).

---

* *Caesar's strategic choice of location also stood the test of time. Nearly two thousand years later, American troops marching into Nazi Germany first crossed the Rhine at Remagen, a mere 12 miles north of the location of Caesar's bridge.*

MILEPOST: SEPTEMBER 28, 1989

A Case Study in Crisis Leadership

Address to the Young President's Organization, White Plains, New York

I've been asked to tell you what it was like during our recent five-and-a-half-year series of crises—to tell you what we learned about operating in a crisis.

A few years ago, I took the Advanced Management Course at the Harvard Business School. As you know, they use the case-study method.

Suppose you are a student at Harvard. The professor walks in, and hands you a piece of paper on which is written: "You have just been named CEO of one of the world's largest oil companies. The company has been dealt an unjust judgment in the biggest lawsuit in history, and owes the plaintiff $10.5 billion. You face the prospect of taking your company into bankruptcy. And as you emerge, you will face a challenge from a well-known corporate raider. Meanwhile, your stockholders, your employees, your customers and your suppliers are relying on you to lead them out of the difficulties." The professor turns to you and says, "O.K. What are you going to do?"

That's essentially the position we found ourselves in here when this management took over in January 1987.

Today, we've put those problems behind us. We've completed a $7 billion restructuring. We've been tested in the fires. We're leaner. We're smarter. And we're well on our way to becoming the kind of company we want to be.

I know I don't have to recite again all the steps we went through. You know what we did. You want to know why we did it. How we did it. And what we learned.

One basic thing we learned might surprise you.

That was: What we did was no different from what you and all good business leaders do every day—exercising leadership:

  ▪ Having a clear concept of your goal.
  ▪ Having confidence in your abilities and those of your people.
  ▪ Making the tough decisions.

■ Staying one step ahead of your opponents.
■ And taking the heat when things don't work out.

True, events were amplified and accelerated during our crises. The numbers had more digits. The publicity was intense. But the principles were the same. And they all require leadership to work.

What are those principles?

I took a moment the other day, and jotted them down.

There are, I believe, eight aspects of leadership that were vital during our crisis, as they are in every business situation. They are:

1. Decision-making.
2. Advisers.
3. Delegation of authority.
4. Ability to operate along several parallel paths at once.
5. Employee morale.
6. Public relations.
7. Negotiating.
8. Personal mental and physical fitness.

Each one figured in our coping with the challenges of the past five and one-half years.

I'll start with *decision-making*.
I used to think there was a right way to do something, and a wrong way. It's not that simple. My experience has taught me that there may be 50 or 100 ways to skin a cat. A lot of choices. A lot of decisions.

Moreover, the hard decisions aren't black-and-white, good and bad. Those are easy. The hard decisions are gray: Good versus better, or bad versus worse. If we do "a," will it cost us less than if we do "b?" And quite often, one decision naturally leads to another.

For example, the decision to take Texaco into Chapter 11 flowed from the Texas judgment. It was the best decision from a strategy standpoint; it was the only way we could have had a chance to obtain a fair hearing on this unthinkable miscarriage of justice—which went against the weight of the evidence and the opinions of most legal experts, business leaders and editorial writers. It was also the best decision from a financial standpoint; it saved our stockholders hundreds of millions of dollars, relative to our alternatives.

We knew it would not be the best decision from the standpoint of being exposed to a takeover. We were well aware it could lead to a battle. Which it did. And we knew it would be tough on morale—certainly on our employees, and also on us as leaders. Many of us in top management had worked all our lives in this company, and the first thing we were doing was taking it into Chapter 11.

But even with these questions, it was the right thing to do.

The positives outweighed the negatives. So we bit the bullet, and filed for protection.

Another example: The decision to wage a proxy fight after coming out of Chapter 11. We had other options. We could have made concessions that would possibly have delayed or avoided a fight, but would have been harmful to the long-term interests of the company. So we decided to force a showdown. We knew we were facing the possibility of losing the proxy fight. But we knew that winning would probably end the period of unrest and uncertainty, and let our people concentrate on building the business. We believed that delay did not guarantee eventual success.

In each case, we had to be flexible, quick to adapt. External events over which we had no control changed our situation overnight.

These were tough decisions. But tough decisions are the price of leadership. And once you make them, you have to stick with them, and be comfortable with them. You cannot waste your time and energy second-guessing yourself. That creates confusion in your organization, and shakes the confidence of all about you.

One leader who knew that well was President Truman. I didn't agree with him on all of the issues. But he sure knew how to make a tough decision, then put it behind him and get a good night's sleep.

The way I saw it when we took over, Texaco was in a swamp. Waste deep in the Big Muddy. There were probably a number of paths out. We had to choose a course of action—and fast. It wasn't straight. It wasn't neat. There were brambles and branches in our way. And it may not have been the best way out; we'll never know. But it got us out of the swamp. And that's what counted.

The second element of leadership in our crisis was *dealing with advisers*.

Inside the company, we assembled a first-rate team. Talented officers and directors. Men and women with experience, vision, high ethical standards, and courage.

Outside the company, we retained the very best: Three major law firms, two top public relations firms, and two investment banking firms.

We had excellent advice. And plenty of it. But that can be a problem: choosing some good advice, rejecting other, also good advice—and synthesizing advice from various sources. This requires having your own plan clearly in mind, and looking beyond the immediate crisis, at the long term.

And only the company's leaders can make these decisions. Turning decision-making over to outsiders—no matter how capable they may be—is not best for the company. The company's leaders are the best judges of what is right for the company. They have the most knowledge about it. And they have the company's short- and long-term interests at heart.

The third principle we relied on was *good delegation of authority*.
Let's face it, no matter what your personal abilities are, no individual can do it all. Throughout our crises, we took a team approach to the twin challenges of keeping the company's business activities steaming ahead on course, and at the same time defending ourselves against the opposition's broadsides—while getting off a few well-aimed rounds ourselves.

> **These were tough decisions. But tough decisions are the price of leadership.**

During the crises, we assigned our top people to two special committees, to make sure that both important jobs were being done. I'll tell you more about that in a moment.

We also gave a mandate to the operating departments. It was their job to keep their businesses going, while others fought the current challenges. We had to make sure that we kept our businesses healthy, to provide the resources needed to fight our present battles, and to make sure that we would have a viable company to build on when we emerged from the battle.

Even while we were managing our crises, we never skimped on spending for research, advertising, or vital development of our business properties. That paid off.

Basic research for our exciting new System 3 gasolines—which aid the performance of both new and older cars—was done during the worst of our troubles. This enabled us to launch System 3 quicker, helping Texaco to recover more quickly.

In May 1987, when we were just into bankruptcy, we spent $23 million to buy and refurbish a coker in Bakersfield.

The fourth element of crisis leadership we needed was the ability to *operate along several parallel paths at once* — in other words, to keep several balls in the air at the same time. Again, here is a case of doing what good leaders have to do in the normal course of running their companies. It's just that we had to do it faster, and while juggling more issues.

I mentioned our two top management committees a moment ago — the ones we formed to guide the company through our continuing crises. We set up two committees of senior managers:

■ The "D" or Defense Committee, to fight the current battles.
■ And the "R" or Restructuring Committee, to plan and lay the groundwork for the new Texaco that we were confident would emerge from those battles.

Setting up the two committees allowed us to do both things simultaneously.

The fifth element of our crisis leadership was *employee morale*.
Employees are key to executing the leader's plans. If their morale falls, company effectiveness is crippled.

As Casey Stengel once said, after winning a pennant: "I couldn't have done it without the players!" Well, a business leader can't do it without his or her team members, either. Our employees suffered greatly during the suit, bankruptcy and the proxy fight. But they continued to perform magnificently throughout the entire nightmare. I'm very proud of them.

There are three essentials of leadership in maintaining employee morale:

■ One is by example. As tough as things may be, regardless of how you feel, you've got to keep your chin up and a smile on your face. You may be worried, but you've got to exude confidence, or you cannot instill it in others. I don't mean faking it. Throughout our crises, our top managers exhibited confidence because we genuinely had confidence — in our abilities, in our people, and in the justness of our cause. We knew we'd eventually prevail — even though we weren't always sure exactly how we'd do it!

▓ Second, we also bolstered morale with appropriate rewards. We kept merit increases coming, even during the bankruptcy. We maintained our good benefits, and now we're improving them.

▓ Third, good communication also is essential for maintaining employee morale. You have to fight the tendency to draw the wagons into a circle, or crawl into a hole.

It is vital to have full and open communication with your employees, because you must control what is being said. If you do not communicate, employees' only sources of information are outside your control: rumors, the media, or your opponents. The worst thing that can happen is for your employees to get the so-called "inside story" of their company on the evening news.

Also, communication has to be two-way. A good leader must be as willing to listen as to talk. You learn a lot that way. But employees won't talk to you unless you're open and receptive.

To communicate throughout crises at Texaco, we used letters to employees, hot lines, videotaped messages, and large and small face-to-face meetings.

Showing up in person seemed to help morale. In early 1987, Al DeCrane and I toured many company facilities. We spoke to 4,000 employees in Houston, and several thousand in New York, London, Los Angeles, Tulsa, Denver, and several other locations. And at the height of our difficulties, we held a company picnic, to thank employees and their spouses for their loyalty, and reassure them as to their future.

An added point: It's important not to forget your employees' spouses: They share the stress of uncertain times, and can help the employee weather them. They can be formidable allies. We worked to keep them on our side.

The sixth element that we found important during our difficulties was *good public relations*.

Over time, the oil business has not performed this function well. Our public relations effort was abysmal a decade ago. But, like many companies, we have learned how important it is. And we are getting better at it.

Just as we knew that internal communication with our employees was vital, we also knew the importance of communications with our external constituencies: stockholders and Wall Street; customer and suppliers; opinion leaders, including the press; our peers in other companies; and the voting public and their government officials.

This required choosing our PR advisers and supporting them, identifying our targets, and then, the communicating itself. We retained the best professionals we could find, on staff and in outside agencies. Then we not only provided adequate money, but equally important, adequate access to our time.

With their help, we identified the constituents we wanted to reach, then determined the most efficient way to reach each of them. This is vital: We knew we must target those where our message would have the greatest impact, so as not to waste our efforts.

We mounted a carefully planned, closely coordinated, world-wide campaign to tell our story:

- Direct mail to important constituencies.
- Personal phone calls to key leaders and opinion-makers.
- Videotaped messages.
- A lot of face-to-face meetings with stockholders. During the proxy fight of 1988, Al and I visited some 20 cities in 15 days, and talked in person to the holders of more than 100 million shares.
- And interviews with the print and broadcast media.

Many of our senior people, including myself, took speech and interview training. We appeared on McNeil-Lehrer, CNN, FNN and several talk shows. Some lessons we learned:

- I found I prefer to appear live, rather than on tape. That way, remarks are not subject to editing, which can distort them. But we did not refuse a recorded interview, just so long as it was done by a responsible journalist.
- We also learned to control the agenda when being interviewed. It's best to go into an interview with three or four simple things you want to say. Then adapt the interviewer's question to it. It's important not to appear to ignore the question. But usually you can find a bridge to what you want to say.

The communication itself was hard work and time-consuming. And there's always a temptation to neglect it for other, more pressing matters. But we knew how important it was to get our message out to our publics.

One problem we had regarding public relations was a conflict with openness. We wanted to communicate our strategic goals. But in these emergencies, we could not reveal our tactics. So we often could not be as open as we'd have liked.

The seventh principle that proved important in our crises was *a negotiating plan.*
Here we found that preparation was everything.

There's an old saying among trial lawyers that you should never ask a question in court to which you don't know the answer. It's the same in negotiating: Never make an offer if you are not prepared for the response. From our experience, preparation means:

- Having a plan or objective in mind before we go into negotiations.
- Marshalling our arguments, and the facts and figures to back them up, before we start negotiating.
- Agreeing on alternative and fallback positions, in advance, to respond to any contingency.
- Remaining flexible. As I mentioned earlier, we sometimes had to recast our whole position overnight, based on outside events.
- Listening, very carefully, to our advisers, our friends, and—this is important—to our adversaries.

> **The spoils don't necessarily go to the smartest negotiator. Sometimes they go to the one with the most stamina.**

Finally, there is *preparing yourself mentally and physically.*
This is the eighth and final element of leadership that was vital during our crises at Texaco—good personal mental and physical fitness.

Negotiation is hard work. And the spoils don't necessarily go to the smartest negotiator. Sometimes they go to the one with the most stamina. Three of the major agreements we've negotiated have come after all-night sessions: the acquisition of Getty; the settlement of the suit; and the settlement with Icahn.

So you often need mental and physical strength and stamina in difficult negotiations. Leadership is a stressful pursuit at best. In a crisis, it can take a terrible toll on an individual. Any student of history knows what the stress of major events did to Woodrow

Wilson at the end of the First World War, and to Franklin Roosevelt at the end of the Second. And because their physical health failed, they were unable to finish what they had set out to do.

Texaco's crisis period lasted five and one-half years. During that period, hundreds of Texaco people bore up well under the stress and strain of extraordinary events. Most of us kept our health through that long nightmare.

I can't speak for all of them. But for myself, I recognized that we were in a marathon, not a sprint. I knew we would be under great stress for a long time. So I found that it was important to eat right, exercise, get a good night's sleep, and get away from the problems of the office periodically—if only for a few hours. I hunt in the winter and play golf in the summer. I go with good friends. And if I wanted to talk about Texaco, they'd listen. If not, they wouldn't bring it up.

It's also important to have a spouse who will listen. I've been very lucky in that, and if I've had any success in my career, much of the credit goes to my wife, Mary.

Texaco has come through a trial by fire. We're stronger, leaner, more innovative than ever before. We're ready to move on.

Despite the setbacks, we've won the war. Texaco has survived, and has enormous potential. Now we've got to win the peace, and fulfill that potential.

That's a different sort of leadership challenge. It requires different skills and approaches. Now, there is tremendous adrenaline flowing through our people at Texaco. We in management must ask ourselves:

- How do we harness it?
- How do we avoid a letdown?

My belief: By setting out a clear vision, with strategies to achieve it.

We do have a clear vision: To be one of the most admired companies in the world. And we have a new strategic plan, which contains a number of strategic initiatives to build on our operating strengths and technology. There are additional opportunities to enhance our business prospects and results. And they set us apart from the competition as leaders, innovators and creators. They are especially important in achieving our vision.

We also have significantly changed our corporate culture. It is much more open. We are listening more. We are improving our rewards, benefits and training. We are encouraging initiative, risk-taking, innovation, entrepreneurship.

One of our vital strategic initiatives concerns quality. We have an on-going, company-wide program to instill high quality into everything we do—all our products, services and operations.

So the challenge to our future leadership is just beginning. But we're in a bright new era.

■

Retrospective on working with advisers

Looking back at the Young Presidents speech with the advantage of hindsight, I think I could have added a little more candor on the process of working with advisers—with lawyers, for example.

Three things have I learned about lawyers. They work in relays; they want you to stay up all night; and they like to eat.

Although my own stamina was pretty good, it did seem to me during our crisis that we engaged in a race that was more like a marathon than a 100-yard dash. That meant we should save some strength for when it was really needed. Particularly because some all-night sessions were unavoidable, it was a good idea to have the sleep tank full. So most nights I would pack it in at 7:30 p.m., and be back at it at 7 a.m. the next morning.

On one late-night session, which took place in my office at Texaco, things seemed to be moving along toward an agreement. People were getting tired and anxious to get the deal signed and go home. Then what should appear but an enormous order of take-out Chinese food.

"Who the _____ ordered that?" I exploded—knowing full well it was the lawyers. "Now they'll get their blood sugar back up, just like my hunting dogs, and we'll *never* get done!"

Sure enough, our now-refreshed group of negotiators got a second wind, and it was not until 7:05 a.m. the next morning that we finally signed the deal. But maybe I shouldn't have complained. Despite the long hours—and perhaps even because of the Chinese food—the deal was a good one. It was extremely complicated, but later events proved it fair to both parties. It was carried out to the letter.

4

The Ethical Dimension of Business Leadership

L eadership is implemented through skills and techniques that can be learned—from the best ways to work with advisers, to the best approach in negotiations. But at another level it depends upon something from within, something spiritual—a firm and sure sense of the ethical imperatives that must govern the choices we make as we shoulder our responsibilities.

In the most fundamental sense, this is what separates a leader from a boss. A leader is guided by values, which he or she projects into ethical standards for the whole organization.

Make no mistake: ethics are as important in the leadership of business as in any other field—if not more so. Business involves:

- The leveraging of human and physical resources,
- to produce goods and services that enhance the quality of life,
- while providing employment,
- and while paying a return on the savings of those who have invested in the business.

Each of those factors is a moral good. Each imposes an ethical responsibility.

Ethical conduct is a hallmark of great leaders throughout history. No leader can aspire to greatness without a firm code of ethical behavior, which will guide every move. The leader sets not just the course, but also the tone for any organization. Leaders who have practiced an inattention to ethical behavior have been the downfall of more than one company.

And ethical leadership must be exercised *by example*. A leader, today, is always on stage—and must be willing to live his life in a spotlight that will expose him, warts and all. Leadership by moral example is a powerful force in the successful operation of a corporation; its absence will lead to failure.

The fact that there is a compelling need for an ethical compass to guide the exercise of leadership does not mean, of course, that it's easy to find and follow this compass. Today it is popular wisdom to equivocate, to bemoan the various shades of gray that many ethical decisions come packaged in. We may think we live in an uncertain world where absolute morals no longer exist—but I suspect that leaders have been voicing that same complaint forever, and that issues of right versus wrong, bad versus worse, and good versus better are not just recent-day concerns.

Precisely because these issues are longstanding and complicated ones, it is only by constantly rethinking them—constantly challenging ourselves to do better—that we can hope to employ ethical standards that are equal to the responsibilities we bear.

It was with this thought in mind that I accepted an invitation to present a paper on ethics in business to an Institute on Values which had been convened at St. Paul's School in Concord, New Hampshire.

Meeting in the lovely library by a lake, and in the shadow of the school's impressive Chapel, were the heads of 42 secondary schools located in the United States, Canada and Great Britain. The group examined the issues associated with the existence of a moral standard in light of the many changes occurring in our world. In retrospect it seems somewhat presumptuous for me to have been speaking on ethics to such an erudite group of educational leaders, clerical and lay alike. But once the subject was joined, the discussion of ethical issues existing in the business world proved very thought-provoking, and not so far removed from academe at all.

MILEPOST: JUNE 18, 1991

Ethics and Values Work for Business

Institute on Values, St. Paul's School, Concord, New Hampshire

———

I am somewhat over-awed, facing this audience of influential educators. But I feel that this interchange, involving a practicing businessman, is extremely important.

I cannot think of a subject more crucial to the future of civilization than that of the values we live by. Especially at this juncture of history.

In my view, the Western world faces a major crisis of values. It stems not so much from the struggle between good and evil, but rather from the difficulty of defining what is good.

Most people want to do "good." But there are certainly wide differences of opinion on what constitutes success in this regard.

There are ethical, principled advocates on both sides of today's most divisive disputes, ranging from the issue of obscenity and government funding of the arts, to abortion and the rights of the unborn, to free speech on college campuses.

So the subject of our institute here at St. Paul's is both timely and important. That's especially so for you, who are charged with educating the leaders of the 21st Century.

Having spent almost my entire career in business, I felt that the most useful contribution I could make to our institute today would be to address the subject of values as they apply to the world of business.

There are four major points I want to make.

First: That business is an essential component of a free society—one that's both necessary and desirable, if society is to function efficiently and best serve the people.

Second: That the creation of wealth by invention, exploration, investment and training—ethically carried out—is a constructive function.

Third: That business runs best when it runs ethically—that unethical practices are self-destructive, and will eventually ruin a business.

And fourth: That it is an important function of the academic world to provide the ethical, as well as the intellectual, grounding of the business leaders of the future.

The starting point for me is that I feel strongly that business is a worthy and ethical undertaking—one that benefits our society and provides psychic as well as material rewards for the individual.

An obvious social benefit of business is the creation of wealth and jobs, which are fundamental to the welfare and advancement of society.

In the last 45 years, since I was a student here at St. Paul's, the population of the world has doubled. Had the number of jobs and the output of goods and services not also grown, one can easily see how economic stagnation, and the possible social disruption stemming from it, could have ensued.

> **Business in a free-market economy encourages and rewards individual talent, creativity, and even courage.**

But, as important as the quantity of jobs, goods and services is, I honestly feel that business makes an even greater contribution to the common good in another dimension: in the quality of people's lives.

Most advances in medicine, transportation, food production, the dissemination of knowledge—even education—were created or developed by private industry. Everything from the electric light bulb to lasers, from antibiotics to the word processor.

Moreover, business in a free-market economy encourages and rewards individual talent, creativity, and even courage. It's been said that, whenever you see a successful business, someone once made a courageous decision. I believe that's true.

If we accept that business is a necessary and desirable component of a free society, it's also fundamental that business must operate in accordance with the highest ethical standards.

That's the way it functions in firms that survive, and therefore serve society most effectively. I've seen that throughout my career.

There are several good, practical reasons why this is true.

One is that in a free market, business operates at the sufferance of society. The record shows, again and again, that the company that acts contrary to society's interests will soon find itself out of favor with consumers and their representatives in government.

It's obvious that periods of excess in business, such as the late 19th Century or the Roaring Twenties, have historically been followed by periods of restrictive legislation.

Unethical practices also endanger one of a business's most precious assets, its reputation. A good reputation does more than make you feel good. It is a real—a measurable—asset. And it can take years to build up a reputation, but only one careless or foolish act to destroy it. Just think of the headlines of the last few years, and a number of prominent company names will come to mind.

The fact is, ethical values actually help a business compete. That's because they provide the rules that business needs to function effectively in a free marketplace.

Chaos and instability are the enemies of sound business operations. Commerce and industry function best under conditions of fair competition and order, where everybody knows the rules.

Adhering to ethical values also makes a company stronger and more efficient. For example, in the oil industry, we're facing major environmental challenges worldwide. To the extent we can lead the way to solving these problems to the greatest benefit of the public, consumer and taxpayer, we will be seen as a valuable part of our society. This will take investment, research and communications skills, but use of these skills can solve one of the greatest challenges of the day.

Ethical values become even more valuable to a company during a crisis. Some business people operate under the illusion that ethical values are all fine and dandy when things are going well—but when a crisis occurs, ethics go out the window, and anything goes. Nothing could be further from the truth. When management is beset with unprecedented or overwhelming challenges, solid values serve as beacons in the storm—or perhaps more relevant to the Middle East, guideposts in the shifting sands.

A firm foundation in visions and values helps managers make the tough decisions, and do it under pressure. One need not reinvent the wheel for every new situation.

The ethical issues business managers face go well beyond simple questions like bribes or payola, or insider trading. They're easy to deal with, because they're wrong, and that's that.

But what about the questions of applying the same standards of equal opportunity or product safety or environmental protections around the world? Ideally, we strive to do that. But levels of industrial development and education, or even climatic conditions, often differ. So they may require different approaches. Laws and customs also vary from country to country, and sometimes conflict with one another.

Social standards change over time, too, and we have to change with them, if we're going to do the right thing. These involve such business issues as maternity leave for employees, which was rare just a few years ago. Today, it's common and desirable.

There are also those questions of defining what is the "good" thing to do. Does a company do more to end apartheid in South Africa by closing down its operations and leaving? Or should it stay and attempt to work for the end of apartheid from within?

What about closing down an unprofitable refinery? At Texaco a couple of years ago, we had to decide what to do with an outmoded refinery at Port Arthur, Texas. Shutting it down might have been good from the shareholders' viewpoint. But it would have devastated the local economy.

I'm proud that we decided to make a substantial investment in upgrading that refinery, and today it is profitable. So we were able to do right for both sides in this question. But on a lot of issues, we have to choose one course over the other.

In coming years, business will face even more complex issues of social significance, and on a scale never faced before. Issues of environmental protection, of the impact of business decisions on the surrounding community, of equal opportunity and affirmative action, of job and product safety, of national security, and many more.

And what business does will become even more significant to the broader society. The world marketplace continues to integrate and the free market system to expand, with the decline of Marxism and the development of third-world economies.

Therefore, the ethical values of the business leaders who are in school today will be of vital importance in determining what kind of a world the future will see.

Because ultimately, in a business, it is the leader who is responsible for setting the ethical tone of the organization, whether that organization is an entire corporation, a division, or a smaller team.

That means the business leaders of the 21st Century must be individuals with a sound ethical foundation, a broad view of history, the ability to communicate, and a profound understanding of their company's place in society.

In other words, the world will need business leaders who share the very values that our schools are dedicated to fostering.

I happen to believe that leadership can be taught. That not all leaders are "born leaders." And generally, that the higher one rises in an organization, the less important specific skills become, while the ability to communicate and inspire becomes more important.

Whatever the reason, today's worlds of education and of business tend to be like ships that pass in the night—heading in opposite directions, each unaware of the other.

As a result, business is too often denied the best students from our best schools, students with that extra dimension of intellectual and ethical development.

The core of my message to this group today is this: Business is too important to our society to leave its leadership to any but the best intellects and the most ethical individuals.

> **Business is too important to our society to leave its leadership to any but the best intellects and the most ethical individuals.**

My hope is that, by working together more closely—as we are today—leaders of business and leaders in education can find ways of building greater understanding of each other's mission, and thereby getting our two ships headed in the same direction.

Why hasn't this been the case up to now? I think part of the problem is that business generally rates poorly in public esteem. Especially the oil companies.

One poll taken after the Iraqi invasion of Kuwait last year showed that 84 percent of the respondents believe that the oil companies were making excess profits by taking unfair advantage of the situation. It wasn't true, but a lot of people thought it was.

Additionally, the very idea of profit is often denigrated as somehow unethical by people who should know better.

Last fall, when gasoline prices shot up after the invasion, a senator from Connecticut called for a law to, in his words, "encourage the oil industry to put patriotism before profits."*

This was in spite of the fact that we could demonstrate, with facts and figures, that gasoline prices actually rose less than the price we had to pay for the crude oil from which we make gasoline.

---

* *His comment echoed the accusations of another senator in Washington in the 1970s, who castigated the oil industry for "obscene profits." Public attack on oil companies remains popular with politicians, although it does nothing to stimulate production or moderate demand.*

I suppose the senator's statement was good politics. But surely he and others know that, without profits, a business could not continue to exist. The money needed for investment would dry up, and with it, capital for research and jobs.

One only has to hear about the hardships faced by the laid-off employees of companies like General Motors, Eastern Airlines or the U.S. steel industry to realize just how important profits are — not only to Wall Street, but to Main Street.

The portrayal of business in the media and in literature has not enhanced its reputation among idealistic young students, either.

> **Most of all... business needs to ensure that its conduct adheres to high ethical standards. That demands leadership.**

Fictional characters in business and commerce—from Shylock in *The Merchant of Venice*, to Ebenezer Scrooge and J.R. Ewing—are usually depicted as evil, or at least venal stereotypes. They have hardly an ethical or compassionate bone in their bodies.

You may know the comic strip, "Doonesbury." It's drawn by a St. Paul's graduate, Gary Trudeau.

Recently, one of the characters, looking for a job in advertising, tells how he "did spots selling Reagan to black voters, created an R.J.R. pitch to entry-level smokers, and did a big campaign for Universal Petroleum." The other character replies, "You sure sold out a lot."

Well, I get a kick out of Doonesbury. But I don't understand how one could view petroleum production as "selling out." Not if you drive a car, fly in airplanes, or use central heating and electric power. Yet that's not an unusual view of my industry in the media.

I'm also reminded of one of those classic cartoons from the "New Yorker." It shows a group of smug-looking executive types, sitting around a conference table. And the leader says, "Of course, honesty is one of the better policies!"

That's amusing. But sadly, it is a stereotype that too many people have of business.

Now, I'm not blaming others for this. There's no denying that business has to take much of the responsibility for its reputation. Misdeeds on Wall Street, the savings and loan scandal, and various environmental and safety incidents are all too familiar to us.

But certainly, they are the exception! And business has to do a better job of making that known to the public.

Most of all, however, business needs to ensure that its conduct adheres to high ethical standards. That demands leadership. And for the future, it will depend on the caliber of the people who will be tomorrow's business leaders. They must be the best.

So we come back to the question: How can we encourage more of the brightest of our students to consider careers in business? I have some specific ideas.

For one thing, our schools can reassess their courses and teaching methods, to determine if their best students are being encouraged to view business as a desirable career option.

I urge you to ask yourself if business is being depicted in your school as a productive, fulfilling career alternative. Or are the old stereotypes simply being recycled?

Also, is your curriculum related, where appropriate, to concepts and issues that would be useful to a student who chooses a career in business? That could help present business as more appealing and exciting to young people.

I'm not advocating vocational education in your schools. But I am advocating serious exposure to math, chemistry and physics, in addition to the already strong communications skills.

I know from my own personal experience that the foundations for those disciplines have to be laid before a student enters college.

For its part, business can help by increasing its contacts with students, on campus as well as through summer jobs and internships.

We can work to see that business is associated in students' minds with freedom of inquiry, an open mind and the encouragement of innovation and individual enterprise.

Business also has to genuinely encourage those qualities of inquiry, innovation and individual enterprise among its employees. Because the students who go to work for companies are going to return to campus, and tell their younger brothers and sisters what it's really like, working in the business world.

I'm reminded of something Harry Truman once said. As you may know, Truman didn't have the benefit of a college education. But he loved books, and spent hours in the library.

Truman believed that, in his words, "Men make history and not the other way around. Progress occurs when courageous, skillful leaders seize the opportunity to change things for the better."

Perhaps it is time that we, the men and women who are leaders of our professions, seize this opportunity, and work to teach the visions and values—the moral standard—upon which our freedom depends.

Ethics in practice

One of our modern buzzwords is "pragmatic." It can be a compliment, if it is used to suggest a down-to-earth understanding of the situation. But being "pragmatic" cannot mean bending the ethical fences a little, on the grounds that everybody does it.

Nowhere are leadership skill and ethical behavior more inextricably woven together than in the armed services, where life and limb are at stake—where one's personal ambitions, one's unit's mission, and the overriding interest of one's country all come into play. Having a firmly focused moral compass is absolutely essential to a career in the military.

While the civilian leader has an enormous responsibility for the social and economic welfare of his various constituencies—often in conflict, one with another—the military leader holds in his hands the very lives of those entrusted to his command. Often the military leader must act *now*; discussion groups, advisers and contemplative time are not available. The military leader's reactions must be perfectly tuned to doing "the right thing," and to knowing in the wink of an eye what *is* "the right thing." And a military leader is fully accountable for what he or she does, to an extent rarely seen in the civilian world.

Naval Regulations, for example, state bluntly that "the responsibility of a commanding officer for his or her command is absolute." They add that during combat, "the commanding officer shall engage the enemy to the best of his or her ability." And finally, "if it becomes necessary to abandon the ship, the commanding officer should be the last person to leave."

Military tradition sees a big distinction between *accountability*, and "accepting responsibility"—a distinction many people today are unaware of. "Accepting responsibility" these days seems to mean admitting you were wrong, and moving on. Accountability means suffering the consequences of your failures. In 1757, Admiral John Byng of the British Royal Navy was put to death by firing squad for "failure to do his utmost" in attempting to relieve the French siege of Minorca. Today many people would recoil in horror at the idea of suffering *any* consequences—let alone execution—for failing to do their utmost. But that's accountability.

The U.S. Naval Academy understands this point completely and has very successfully made ethical training an integral part of its leadership curriculum. The Academy seeks to make habitual those actions that are "good." "Good" habits are developed through drill and practice, beginning with small issues and growing to large issues.

When I was asked by the Academy to speak to some 600 midshipmen at the Academy's 35th Annual Foreign Affairs Conference, therefore, I found it both a real honor, and a rare opportunity to think through the ways in which ethics impact business.

MILEPOST: APRIL 19, 1995

The Ethics of International Business

35th Annual U.S. Naval Academy
Foreign Affairs Conference, Annapolis, Maryland

━━━━━━━━━━━━━

I have been asked to talk to you about ethics in business, especially in international business. When the subject is ethics, there's always a danger of preaching.

You know, there's a little story about President Coolidge. Calvin Coolidge was a notoriously laconic man—so much so that he was nicknamed "Silent Cal." Well, one Sunday morning, when Silent Cal went off to church by himself and came back home, his wife asked, "Was the sermon good?"

"Yes," he answered.

"What was it about?"

"Sin."

"Well," she said, "What did the minister say?"

"He was against it."

Well, we're all against sin, and we're all for ethics. But for a discussion of ethics to be productive, I believe it has to be practical. It has to relate to the real world. It has to relate to the way business is really done.

We know it's not a perfect world out there. We know it's not a perfect world in here. But something deep inside us craves the right and the good. It's something deep within human nature and within the human heart.

There are very, very few of us who, when we stray from the straight and narrow, when we do something unkind or dishonest or unethical or just morally weak, do not feel uneasy, anxious— I'll say it: plain lousy.

We can cover up the feeling—with rationalizations, with distractions, or even with alcohol or drugs, as some people do. We can run from it. We can run. But we can't hide.

It's not just fear of punishment. It's not just fear of getting caught. The very fact that we have something to hide from other people means we do not admire the sight of it ourselves.

Although there is much in our environment, and even in our genes and our hormones that pushes us in the wrong direction, I would like to believe that the human soul is never at rest, never at peace with itself, unless it is doing good.

But what about that imperfect world out there? What about the people who seem to get ahead by bending the rules, or breaking the rules, or trampling the rules? In an imperfect world, isn't it necessary to break the rules just to keep up with the other rule-breakers?

Isn't this a world where the J.R. Ewings as in "Dallas"—or the Gordon Gekkos, if you saw the movie "Wall Street," or the Amanda Woodwards, if you watch "Melrose Place"—isn't this a world where such people are the real winners?

That was what Niccolo Machiavelli taught four hundred years ago. That was what the sophists said in the time of Socrates. It's not a new argument. It's a very old argument. The unjust argument, it's called.

But I am here to tell you that it's a phony argument, a misleading argument, a totally shortsighted argument.

And I am saying this on the basis of many, many years spent, not only in the Navy, but in another of the world's toughest and riskiest businesses—the oil business. No business for wimps. And I am saying this after having been fortunate enough to enjoy a little of what the world is pleased to call success.

Ethics work.
That's my first message for you today. I believe it as strongly as I believe any lesson I've learned in life. I believe it not just as a matter of faith, but because I've experienced it first-hand.

I've seen the results when you make it a priority to conduct yourself and your business ethically, in conformity with the law and with sound ethical principles. And I've seen the results when people try to cut ethical corners and bend or break the rules in search of some short-term gain. When you look objectively at the concrete results of these two approaches to business, these two approaches to life, there's just no contest. On every score, the ethical approach eventually wins hands down.

You know, contrary to what a lot of people imagine, ethical behavior is the rule, and not the exception, in business, especially American business.

Over the past thirty or so years, unfortunately, we've experienced a massive loss of confidence in our major institutions.

People have a low opinion of the government and politicians. They have a low opinion of the media. And they have a low opinion of business, at least from an ethical standpoint.

In opinion polls, when people are asked to rank professions according to their ethical soundness, business executives are normally ranked about twelfth or thirteenth on the list, well below the clergy, as you might imagine. But also slightly above lawyers— thank Heaven! TV and films may have something to do with this.

In a recent book, *Prime Time: How TV Portrays American Culture*, opinion experts Robert Lichter, Linda Lichter, and Stanley Rothman report that business people in prime time TV dramas are twice as likely to be portrayed as bad guys, and three times as likely to commit crimes, as compared with characters in other professions.

> **On every score, the ethical approach eventually wins hands down.**

The authors found that three out of four shows which depicted business actually being conducted showed it as corrupt and unethical. No other profession was so portrayed. No wonder some people assume that unethical behavior is the rule in business!

But that's drama. In drama you need conflict, you need villains. The badder, the better. That's show business, and that's Hollywood, with all its peculiar biases.

But it's not real business or real life. Let me assure you this common caricature of business is a gross misperception.

Sure, there are bad people and morally weak people in business, just as there are in every other walk of life. But the vast majority of American corporations are run on an ethical basis. They have to be, because among other reasons the costs of unethical practices are too high.

The ethics of American business have been strengthened by a series of laws and reforms over the past twenty years, laws like the 1977 Foreign Corrupt Practices Act, which forbids American corporations from bribing foreign officials.

Now, some people have argued that the Foreign Corrupt Practices Act puts American business at a disadvantage globally, because in fact no other country has such a law.

In many countries today, of course, bribery and kickbacks are still a way of business and a way of life. Today, for example, a French company doing business abroad can bribe a foreign official and deduct the bribe on its tax return. That's true throughout Europe, and most of the world.

An American corporation would violate U.S. law by bribing in the first place, and if convicted, the corporation would be fined and the officers of that corporation could go to jail.

In my experience the Foreign Corrupt Practices Act has not been a hindrance, but a help.

When American businesses are approached by bribe-seeking foreign officials, they can use Nancy Reagan's line, "Just say 'No'." They can say, "Sorry, Charlie, but American law does not permit this, and if we pay you, we are going to get ourselves into real hot water." Such a response gives everybody a face-saving way out.

It turns out that these countries usually need and want our business anyway. Not only do we save the money otherwise spent on bribery, but we avoid the morass of distrust and deceit that almost inevitably follows once the bribing begins.

Shakespeare was right: Deception does weave a tangled web.

> **In the end, honor is not just better—it's also easier.**

Of course, you can succeed for a while by twisting the rules. You can race ahead of the pack, temporarily. But unethical behavior involves a very strenuous juggling act: You've got to keep track of your lies, and the persons you lied to. Your relationships with the people closest to you tend to suffer, because you're living with a lie. All of this is taxing. It takes an enormous amount of energy and generates an enormous amount of anxiety.

In the end, honor is not just better—it's also easier.

We all have something called a reputation, which follows us around as persistently as our own shadows. Companies have reputations, too. In fact, you can actually put a dollar figure on a company's reputation. The value of a concern's shares is determined by its earnings, its cash flow, its dividends—and by its reputation.

You build a good reputation, both as an individual and as a company, not only by being competent at what you do, but by being dependable, by being fair, by being good to the people and customers you deal with, and by telling the truth—in short, by being ethical.

Unethical people and unethical companies eventually develop a reputation for being unethical, and it usually costs them dearly. In the case of some companies, it has destroyed them.

It's hard to keep secrets in this world, harder than many people might imagine, and in the Information Age it's becoming even more difficult to do so. The seeing eye of the media now penetrates into every dark corner. The newspapers of countless countries are filled daily with stories of government or business corruption. In America this scrutiny has been going on for a while, at least since Watergate. But now it's happening abroad, around the globe, to an unprecedented extent.

In the past couple of years, several national governments have been toppled, a number of top corporate executives in various countries have gone to jail, and hundreds of politicians have been driven from office—all because of a growing worldwide public intolerance of corruption. And, I would add, because of the growing power of the media in the Information Age to expose such corruption.

So here is my second point: Today we are in the midst of a global ethics revolution.

There are many aspects to it. One is the growing public revulsion for corrupt business and political practices, which I have just mentioned. Another aspect is the revival of public interest in the question of moral values. You can see it in the success of such books as William Bennett's bestseller, *The Book of Virtues*.

There is a strong sense among many, many people in many different countries today that the standard of both public and private conduct must be raised.

Not only will this make for a better world, but I believe it will help American business. By and large, you may be surprised to hear, American companies are in the ethical vanguard. We're ahead of companies in other countries in our ethical policies and ethical practices.

At Texaco, for example, we have had a set of guiding principles in place since the company was founded in 1902. These principles state in no uncertain terms that we expect the highest standards of moral and ethical conduct throughout the company, and that these standards will be enforced.

We have always done our best to play by the rulebook, at home and abroad.

If other countries now pass new laws and begin to enforce tighter ethical standards on their businesses, companies that already make it a policy to play by the rules can only benefit.

Utopia is still a long way off, of course. But over time, I believe this new worldwide ethical consciousness will improve business practices around the globe. It's almost an inevitable result of the globalization of business itself. If we're trading heavily with each other, if we're investing in each other's countries, it's only going to work well in the long run if we're all guided by the same standards. And I think business people and political leaders and even publics around the globe are beginning to see this.

Now, there are some people who argue that the idea of business itself is unethical. They worry about the consumption of our natural resources. They worry about the environment. They see the modern lifestyle as a destructive to the planet.

I believe there can be a legitimate element to these worries. We have to take prudent steps to protect our environment and our resources. And we do. In the future, we will have to do more.

But I also believe it is a serious mistake to overlook how vital business is today to the health of the planet and to the health of humanity.

First, there is the issue of political health.
Today, according to Freedom House, there are 114 democracies around the globe, up seven from last year. This is a remarkable achievement, especially when you consider that a little over two hundred years ago, there was only one liberal democracy on the planet—the United States of America.

The spread of democracy could not have occurred without the spread of the modern economy, without economic development, which means without business.

Our founding fathers knew this. When Thomas Jefferson wrote the phrase "the pursuit of happiness" in the Declaration of Independence, he was actually adapting a phrase from John Locke, which originally read "the pursuit of property."

Our founding fathers saw free commerce as a powerful force for human liberation, as one of the foundations of a free society. And the past two hundred years have proved them unequivocally correct.

Democracy as we know it depends on the wealth-generating powers of business to guarantee a certain minimum lifestyle and level of economic security and opportunity. Without a healthy economy, it is very difficult for a country to sustain political stability and political freedom—as history has so often proved, even in this century. The turmoil in the former Soviet Union is but one good case in point.

Second, there is the issue of physical health.

Does anyone here imagine that the astonishing advances in medical technology we have seen in the past generation would have been possible without business? Does anyone imagine that the dramatic advances in agricultural technology, which allow us today to feed the whole of the United States and a good part of the rest of the world using just 3 percent of the American work force—does anyone imagine that business had nothing to do with this? Could it be done without engineering disciplines, machinery, and American management?

In a world where millions are still hungry, still lacking basic medical facilities, still struggling for the rudiments of survival, we need business.

Because in the final analysis, it is only the resources and energy and creativity of global business that can pull these vast populations out of poverty and desperation, into a world of development and opportunity and security.

Third, there is the issue of intellectual and spiritual health and growth.

Business is more than money-making. For the past two hundred years it has probably been the chief outlet for human creativity, for invention, for problem solving, for teaching people how to cooperate in achieving great and vital things together.

And I would also go so far as to say that today, business is the chief force knitting this planet together into a global community. The telegraph, the telephone, air travel, radio, television, computers, CNN—none of this would be possible but for business.

As an oil man, I am particularly aware of how oil has revolutionized the planet in the last hundred years—linking human beings together by car, truck, bus, ship, plane. Thanks to oil and the internal combustion and jet engines, the long, hard trek across the Sierra Nevada Mountains, which killed so many of our pioneers 150 years ago, is now just a few hours' drive, or a short plane hop.

We are on the verge of a new level of globalization in human experience, and business is supplying the energy and resources to help us achieve it.

But this new global environment is also bringing new ethical and legal complexity. And this is my third point today.

In a global environment, where there is still a lot of political chaos, corporations face new ethical and legal dilemmas.

I am not one of those who believe that the multinational corporation, as a legal or economic entity, transcends national borders. I believe a multinational corporation is, and should be, a citizen of the country in which it is incorporated, albeit with subsidiaries and affiliates in other countries whose laws must also be obeyed. Texaco is a U.S. company, a Delaware corporation, and as such we always felt bound to be a good citizen, to obey U.S. law. And we have.

But when you're doing business internationally, this duality can get you into some tight spots. It can lead to outcomes that may not be ideal, even for the people you're trying to help.

This is particularly true when the government of the United States seeks to conduct foreign policy by imposing economic sanctions on another country.

We had two particularly tough experiences with sanctions, one in Haiti, and another in South Africa.

In the early nineties in Haiti, without going into all the details, we were caught between our obligation to obey U.S. law and the pressure on our Haitian employees to obey the laws and dictates of their own government. Crime and violence were rampant in the country, and a couple of our Haitian employees were actually killed.

We acted in accordance with our U.S. legal obligations. We ceased the importation of petroleum, and we tried unsuccessfully to withhold payments from the Haitian government. We did our best to coordinate everything closely with the U.S. government, and to minimize the problems on all sides, but sometimes you just cannot win. We obeyed our law; we did the best we could. But it's a pity that others may have suffered because they, like we, got caught in the middle.*

Sanctions can put a multinational corporation and its local employees in a real bind. Most of the time your employees are

---

* *The government of Haiti bought cargoes of petroleum product, imported them into the country, and demanded that our employees distribute them. Oil is a cash business, and thus the proceeds from this distribution went into the company's local bank account. The government then demanded the money so it could buy more cargoes. The only remaining employees, all Haitians, knew of their instructions from headquarters in the U.S. not to pay anything to the government—but then they looked across the desk at officials of their own country's government ordering them to pay. They faced overwhelming pressures to pay, and they paid.*

citizens of the country being sanctioned. In our Haitian subsidiary, all the employees are Haitians.

As a U.S. corporation, you are obligated to obey U.S. law. But your employees have to answer to their own governments. There can be pressure. There can be violence.

Resentment is usually heightened by the fact that other, non-U.S. firms—companies in the same business you are in—are operating normally in the country, because U.S. sanctions don't legally apply to them.

Congress tends to view sanctions as a less violent, less painful way to conduct foreign policy—as a gentler and less risky way to coerce or punish an adversary government than the use of military force. But sanctions are in fact a very blunt instrument. They are rarely painless for the people of the country in question, and they can also be irreversibly damaging to American companies doing business and having employees and fixed investments in the country.

In South Africa, the situation was a little different, but it was also difficult. In South Africa, where we still have an affiliate, Caltex, we made a decision to stay during the sanctions period — even though we faced enormous pressure from some very sincere and well-meaning critics in the U.S. and abroad to get out. (I should make clear that in this matter, as in Haiti, we were scrupulous to avoid violation of U.S. law.)

I still think the decision to stay in South Africa was the right one, even though it was very unpopular in many quarters at the time, and was not a public-relations plus for Texaco. I personally faced numerous, very heated debates at our stockholders' meetings.

It was tough going. But I'm glad we did it. We were setting an example in South Africa. We had pressed for equality in the workplace. We wanted to show how black and white South Africans could work together on an equal basis and get something important done. This was very vital at the time.

We were an island of liberal thinking amid apartheid. We thought we had a mission, a very constructive mission, not only as a successful firm furthering the interests of its shareholders, but also as a force for progress—which our critics obviously didn't understand.

Did the U.S. and Western-imposed sanctions contribute to the recent miraculous transformation in South Africa? Quite possibly. I don't know. But I do know that in the 1980s we helped create a little vision of what the new South Africa might be. And today, when the South African government under President Nelson Mandela is desperately seeking foreign investment, Texaco, through Caltex, is one of the few big international firms that are there, contributing to the new South African economy. Most other big U.S. firms felt they had to get out, and sadly, they haven't come back.

So sometimes the issue of sanctions can have a lot of shades of gray. Sometimes the issue is not just right versus wrong, but one right versus another. The world is a complicated place, and sometimes you simply can't calculate all the angles, or control all the outcomes. That's why, in the end, you have to follow your own conscience.

That's the final message I'd like to leave you with today.

When faced with a tough decision, think the matter over carefully. Reason out the consequences of your actions. But when in doubt, do what, in all humility, you believe to be right. And then, having done so, do not second-guess yourself.

I'd like to leave you with a wonderful remark of Winston Churchill's on exactly this subject.

It comes from his tribute to an opponent on the floor of the House of Commons, in 1940, amid World War II.

"The only guide to a man," said Churchill, "is his conscience; the only shield to his memory is the rectitude and sincerity of his actions.

"It is very imprudent to walk through life without this shield, because we are so often mocked by the failure of our hopes and the upsetting of our calculations; but with this shield, however the fates may play, we march always in the ranks of honor."

Learning it early

Ethics and leadership, a code of moral behavior and the willingness to expose oneself for the good of the whole organization—these ideas are mutually dependent and must be so taught in the development of our young people. Efficiency is not the only thing that counts. One cannot argue that there was not efficient management in the Wehrmacht of Nazi Germany during the 1930s and the 40s, for example. It was the totally amoral direction of those forces, however, that eventually led to their own destruction, as well as to unthinkable pain and suffering around the world.

With great power comes great responsibility. Most people (not all, but most) want more power, or say that they do. But do they really want the responsibility that comes with that power? That is a question that must be answered early on in any career.

I remember a newly minted ensign standing in front of his division on the deck of the destroyer to promulgate the orders of the day—leadership training in action. Many of the people he is addressing know more about the mission at hand than he does, and the wise "old" chief petty officer (who is perhaps 40) has carried out these orders a thousand times before. But our ensign will stand tall, he will speak slowly and clearly, he will confer with the Chief, he will reward in public and chastise in private, and the mess decks will get painted whether they need it or not. When things go wrong, he will accept the responsibility and put them right; when the division earns an "E" for excellence, he will share the credit with his men.

On the long night watches, this ensign finds plenty of time for thought. In clear weather in the middle of the ocean, the galaxies present themselves in all their glory—and no one, certainly not our young officer, can rationally believe that he represents merely an accidental ectoplasm taking a random walk through infinite space. No, he is more than that, and the logic of a moral standard and the existence of an uncaused cause take firm root in his very soul.

Far out on his port bow the watch officer sees the green sidelight of a merchantman on a constant bearing and closing range. "I know we are the privileged vessel, but does *he* know it?" "I wonder if I should call the Captain?" The green light turns to red as the merchantman changes course to starboard and passes port to port. The watch officer sighs with relief.

During carrier qualifications there is suddenly an eerie silence as a torpedo bomber's engine fails on take-off and the plane hits the water off the starboard bow. In ship-handling school, our young officer was taught to turn toward the plane so the ship's stern will swing away. "Right full rudder!"—an agonizing delay, and the stern swings slowly to port: "Rudder amidships!" As the plane passes down the starboard side the pilot is already on the wing waving a "thank you" to the bridge.

In these and countless other ways, leadership is learned— and its ethical exercise becomes habitual. To take the blame when things go wrong, and to share the rewards of success. To answer the phone at 3 in the morning, knowing that it never rings in the middle of the night with good news. To present an unequivocal standard of morality.

These are the lessons to be learned. They can be learned by study of acknowledged leaders, by reading the works of great philosophers, by emulating present-day heroes. But they will take root most firmly when we apply our ethical standards in our practical life—and then learn by first-hand experience that they produce results. That *ethics work*.

5

Corporate Governance: A System for Accountability

Corporate leadership carries with it the trappings of power—squads of good people to direct, a handsome office, perhaps even a corporate plane. But it is important that neither the CEO, nor other employees, nor the public at large be fooled by these trappings into thinking that this is untrammeled power.

For corporate power is a trust. The CEO is and must be accountable to a Board of Directors. And in turn both that board, and the CEO, are accountable to the shareholders, employees, government, and the public.

The system that implements this accountability is what we call corporate governance. And just as with civil government, there is a diversity of views on how this system should be constituted, peopled and organized.

There is no one answer—nor is it always easy to determine if a particular corporation's governance is working. When a company is growing and profitable, almost any system of corporate governance works, or at least seems to do so in the short term. By the same token, when things are going poorly in an industry, no system of corporate governance alone provides an inexhaustible supply of silver bullets to cure whatever needs to be cured. The true test of a company's system of corporate governance comes at other times—when the firm has lost its way within its industry, or when the firm has been jolted by outside forces over which it has no control.

A company's system of corporate governance includes the nature and quality of its relationship and communications with shareholders, employees and the public at large. But the heart of the governance system is the Board of Directors, which is elected to represent shareholder interests, to oversee management and to hold it accountable. In difficult times, when a strong signal from the top is needed, the Board of Directors can either be a tremendous force for the better—or it can keep its eyes firmly shut, and represent a real obstacle to productive change.

Texaco faced a special crisis after 1985, as reported in the first two chapters. Our Board of Directors proved then to be a vital and united force for the changes we made to protect shareholders and to re-engineer the company. And service for many years on the boards of other well-known companies has brought me to the conclusion that no firm is forever free of crisis—that corporate excellence, competitive standing, ethics and reputation are all subjects that will concern any board at some time.

For that reason, a good Board of Directors is like a two-ocean Navy: You had better start building it years before you need it. Good boards do not just appear overnight, nor do they spring fully blown from the mind of some headhunter. They are conceived, nurtured, trained, instructed, advised and rewarded over a period of years so they will be there when they are most urgently needed.

The Board of Directors must above all be the conscience of the company. It must ensure that shareholders' interests are paramount. It must safeguard the company's assets. And it must take particular care to safeguard the company's reputation. For a good reputation is the company's most precious asset—one that takes years of hard work to develop, and one that can be destroyed in an instant by illegal, unethical or merely thoughtless behavior.

A board's role is wide-ranging, which in turn requires individuals of great depth. It has been said that being a corporate director is one position for which no training is required. But the truth is that the director brings his or her whole life's experience to the table. The position requires an ability to learn what it is important to know about a business, and a willingness to study hard, ask questions, form opinions. A director must have the intellectual curiosity to analyze a situation, must know how to raise concerns without being argumentative, and must relate well to fellow board members. The most helpful directors I have seen are those who study the company, ask questions because they really want answers, and provide supportive criticism.

A good director must also appraise the company's top officers, and its major hires and promotions, with a critical eye. Even the best CEO can use help with these decisions, because they are not easy. It's not terribly difficult to assess a candidate's record in his or her current job, of course; but it is both more difficult, and more important, to project how he or she will perform in a new, more demanding position. The attainment of greater authority and responsibility can sometimes change the behavior of the promoted manager.* Management selection is an art as well as a science, and outside directors can therefore often be invaluable in giving the CEO a "second opinion" in these matters.

For an industrial board, an ideal size is 12 to 15 outside directors. Any number much greater than that becomes unwieldy, but a smaller number doesn't allow committee participation without undue time pressure. The majority of directors should be outsiders. It's appropriate to have two or three insiders to add functional expertise and to provide for succession planning.

Some critics of current corporate governance practices have suggested that the offices of chief executive officer and chairman of the board should always be held by different individuals. The theory seems to be that various complementary skills can be brought to bear without too much power being vested in one person: the CEO runs the company while the chairman communicates with the board.

While this system has worked well in some instances, it does not guarantee good performance by itself. I was very fortunate to have served as CEO with an (executive) chairman whose talents complemented my own, during a very difficult period in the history of our company. The system worked well for us because we made it work. It was particularly helpful at a time when there were many balls in the air, each requiring immediate attention. But there is no hard-and-fast

---

* *In this regard, my own inveterate optimism led me several times to make the mistake of believing that known strengths in an individual would more than compensate for known weaknesses. The tiger and the leopard don't often change their stripes and spots.*

rule here; the question of separating the offices of CEO and chairman should be considered based on the situation at hand and the personalities of the available candidates.

Whether the offices are separated or not, there must be no confusion as to who is in charge of what, and there must be clear, timely, complete and honest advice rendered to the board by management.

Board committees are very useful in the areas of nomination, audit, finance, pension, compensation, and public responsibility. Serious or wide-ranging matters, however, should also be discussed by the committee of the whole, so the thought never arises that some members are more equal than others. An executive committee can be maintained for emergencies—but in these days of advanced communications technology, "virtual" meetings of the whole board can be held at almost any time and are generally preferable to the use of an executive committee.

Special focus in recent years has fallen on the compensation committee of the board. Attractive compensation packages are needed to retain high-quality employees. But as firm after firm seeks to pay in the top quartile of its industry or size sector, it is a mathematical certainty that average compensation will increase exponentially. Fair competitive compensation practices can be reflected in the price of the goods or services being sold; overly generous compensation cannot be recovered in the marketplace and is thus unfair both to the shareholders and to the customers. It is incumbent on the compensation committee to insist on performance goals which, if achieved, will inure to the long-term benefit of *all* the shareholders—measured by the rate of change in earnings per share, cash per share, total return to shareholders versus one's competition, and results versus plan.

Given the importance of the company's reputation, a public responsibility committee is increasingly vital to a board's work. It must deal with a spectrum of issues ranging from the environment to diversity in the workplace, from educational philanthropy to the question of a corporation's place in the funding of the arts. Its responsibilities can include shareholder relations, political involvement, women's issues and related subjects.

Boards must not become static. Having a retirement age is a useful rule, although having one below age 72 is wasteful of talent and experience. A director should offer his or her retirement from the board whenever his primary job changes; the board may not accept it, but the other directors should at least have the opportunity to review the situation.

Whatever the exact structure chosen, leadership on a board must be unequivocal. Committees can perform many useful functions by analyzing, reviewing, comparing, and reporting their findings. But great companies are led by great people, not by great committees. In the times of crisis we experienced, when the going really got tough, fifteen pairs of eyeballs swung to one end of the table as though to ask, "OK, friend, what do we do now?" Leadership must be prepared to answer.

Finally, both executives and directors must consciously think through and re-evaluate the governance systems they are employing. Even in the press of ordinary business—let alone in times of crisis—this is not always easy to do.

Sometimes an invitation to speak outside the company about its governance system provides a chance to clarify your thinking on what works and what doesn't, on why and why not. For us, an opportunity of that kind arose in December 1993, with an invitation to address a Corporate Directors Summit held in Toronto.

MILEPOST: DECEMBER 2, 1993

Ensuring That Boards Contribute to Corporate Success

Corporate Directors Summit, Toronto

———

Corporate governance is a hot topic currently. It gets a lot of press, particularly in the areas of compensation and board activism. In my view, there are many misconceptions surrounding the subject. For example, I feel it is dangerous to conclude, as some have, that U.S. firms have lost their edge, that inadequate corporate governance is the villain, and that the large pension funds have a magic key to success. Certainly there have been compensation excesses and management failures, but over-reaction to them entails its own dangers.

So it's important that everyone, business and government alike, consider all sides of this complex issue, and learn everything we can, before adopting radical change.

The relationship among the CEO, top management and the board of directors is a complex and a fascinating subject, which has developed over many decades.

As we know from reading the papers, it continues to evolve. That's due at least partially to the growing presence of big institutional investors. Pension funds, mutual funds and insurance companies now own more than half of publicly held stock in the U.S., vs. only 18 percent just 25 years ago. Increased globalization of business has also played a part. As the dimensions of competition have changed, institutional shareholders have demanded more accountability from management than in the past. And that demand has given rise to definitional issues: ROE, ROIC, total return, public responsibility, etc.

Also, individual investors' greater awareness of issues and events has increased public scrutiny of management on both financial and societal issues.

To deal with these issues, one must consider the question: "What is the objective of a corporation?" Among many and sometimes contradictory factors, it may well be concluded that the objectives of the corporation should be:

- Financial growth.
- Total return to shareholders.
- Competitive return on invested capital.
- Good citizenship.
- And conformance with appropriate strategic plans.

Boards of directors today are much more actively involved in company matters than they used to be. Generally, I think increased board involvement is a positive development in company management. If a board nominee is not prepared to be an active, inquiring, participating director, he or she should decline the offer to serve. But board members who attempt to micromanage, assume management's authority, or exercise authority without attendant responsibility, can be a negative factor.

Demands on the chief executive have multiplied. A broad spectrum of societal issues has become an important matter of everyday business concern (the environment, diversity of workforce, etc.). At the same time, competition has intensified and become global, increasing pressure on management for financial results, raising the stakes on decisions, and narrowing the tolerance for mistakes.

These trends mean the CEO needs all the wise counsel he or she can get. A Board of Directors, composed of able individuals with diverse backgrounds and experience, can be a valuable ally to the CEO. This was certainly the case during our crisis period a few years ago. The backing of our directors, with their counsel, support and friendship, helped management through many a dark hour.

A good board can also be valuable in more normal times, helping to guide a company's approach to important developing issues. In 1989, we established a public responsibility committee of the board. It has oversight responsibility for, among other things, environment, health and safety; workforce diversity; and shareholder and public interest matters throughout the company. This committee has been an effective aid to management in dealing with these complex matters. Appearing with presentations before this committee provides an incentive and a discipline to company employees.

In my view, the important thing in these questions of corporate governance is to strike a balance between too little involvement and too much. In my 16 years on Texaco's board, plus service on the boards of other companies and organizations, I've developed some strong ideas on how to do this most effectively.

We were in the vanguard of companies moving toward more effective director involvement by emphasizing a formal committee structure to allow directors to study issues in depth. The following committees, committee memberships, and highlighted responsibilities have proved effective:

- *Non-Management Committee.* All of the outside directors are members. This committee considers succession, employee-director pay, and other broad issues brought to it by the CEO or other directors.
- *Audit Committee.* All members are outside directors, and the committee reviews all inside and outside audit practices and results.
- *Nominating Committee.* This committee also is composed of outside directors. It is concerned with board membership, proxy committee membership and related matters.
- *Finance, pension, public responsibility committees.* Management and outside directors are members. Their areas of interest are self-explanatory.
- *Executive Committee.* Management and outside directors are members. This committee exists to provide quick action when required.
- *Compensation Committee.* This committee is composed of outside directors. It approves or recommends for approval all forms of executive compensation.

Switching committee assignment and chairmanships among the board members gives the directors broad experience and a sense of involvement.

The basic principle of a successful board/management relationship is openness: Letting the directors and management know what each other is doing; and having a clear conception of what each expects of the other.

We've spelled out the responsibilities of management and directors in black and white. Authorities for management action are specific and approved in detail by the board.

We have assigned in writing several broad areas of responsibility for the CEO and other senior managers:

- First, top management is held responsible for guardianship of corporate ethics and employee morale.

- ▨ Second, top management is expected to provide leadership in a number of areas: Defining the corporate vision and strategy; making sure the company fulfills a responsible corporate role in society; and setting an example for all employees, customers and suppliers.
- ▨ Third, the board expects senior management to serve as proper stewards of the company's assets, by: Producing strong profit performance; planning for management succession; developing management personnel; minimizing surprises; responding quickly to the board's inquiries; and thinking like owners as well as managers.
- ▨ And finally, in dealing with the Board of Directors, executive management is expected to: Help the board's Nominating Committee find board candidates of high quality; conduct well-planned, efficient and interesting meetings; and use the talents of the board wisely, consulting with the board before decisions are made on key issues.

In practice, so that the board can fulfill its responsibilities, the CEO should keep the board well informed, especially in crisis. And management should help the directors understand the company's history and culture, operations and technology.

Let's look at these points in a little more detail:

> **The CEO must always be direct and truthful, even when the news is bad.**

Keeping the board well informed. Board meetings should provide an open and constructive exchange of information, ideas and opinions. Time should be reserved to provide a detailed discussion of ongoing legal challenges and environmental matters, as these areas develop more and more importance. Directors should have the ongoing opportunity to evaluate management, and to meet and observe members of management in a variety of settings. And the CEO should keep the board continually informed, through meetings and by phone and letter. The CEO must always be direct and truthful, even when the news is bad.

Helping directors understand company operations. It's important to arrange familiarization trips for board members to field locations. Over the past few years, we've taken our directors to see our marketing facilities and refineries in Delaware, Texas and Louisiana, and we've also had some of them visit offshore producing operations in the Gulf of Mexico. At other companies where I serve on the board, I've taken similar trips, which have given me valuable insight into those companies, to help me do my job as director. Such visits give directors a chance to see company operations first-hand, build a collegial atmosphere that is important in a well-functioning board, and meet younger operating people on their home turf.

Scope of directors' responsibilities. A director's authority must be balanced by responsibility. The real and perceived authority of a director is enormous. And this fact can have a wide impact inside and outside the company—directors are widely thought of throughout a company as archangels. Their actions are generally limited only by the business judgment rule. But with authority comes responsibility. An acceptance of individual responsibility is a key to director excellence. For example, a director must choose his or her words carefully in all situations involving the company.

> **An acceptance of individual responsibility is a key to director excellence.**

A course between too little and too much board involvement is desired. Thus, definition of and concentration on company performance best enables a board to find this course. We believe tactical and strategic plans should have board understanding and approval. Management should display alternatives, discuss price-volume-demand scenarios and various investment options. Each month, management should show directors the company's performance vs. its tactical plan in detail. The company's performance by functional area vs. major competitors should be shown to the board at least each quarter. This discipline provides directors with an early warning of any potential weaknesses against the stern yardstick of competition. (These competitive reviews are most effective if they compare a wide range of both operations and financial results, in total and in unit terms, against the published performance of competitors.)

Role of outside directors. The most important responsibilities of a board are management development and succession planning. A board must have continued exposure to management talent, both in formal and informal settings. On any board, there are some jobs that ideally should be performed only by outside directors, to ensure the complete independence of their decisions. We believe that the audit, compensation and nominating committees should be made up completely of outside directors.

These functions ideally have staff support both from the company and from outside consultants.

Composition of board. The board should include a majority of outsiders, as distinguished from management directors. Some seats should be filled by insiders, to develop a succession of management. But outsiders are needed to provide both independent opinions and broader perspective.

The board should be diverse and, as a whole, represent all constituents. I'm not talking about tokenism here—a required quota of women, minorities and so forth. I'm talking about a diversity of talent and experience. Selection should be on merit. Thus, one must achieve gender or ethnic diversity without lowering standards. We know that a corporation best succeeds with the approval of the society in which it operates. A competent, diverse board of high quality helps win and maintain this approval.

Requirements for directors. Fulfilling the high expectations we have for our directors is a tall order. Good directors are hard to find. It takes a special kind of individual. So, to help find the right people for the job, we've drawn up a list of criteria for our directors and published them for our shareholders. The prospective director should:

1. Possess the highest personal and professional ethics, integrity and values.
2. Have the education and breadth of experience to understand business problems, and to evaluate and propose solutions.
3. Have the personality to work well with others. That includes depth and a wide perspective in dealing with people and situations.
4. Respect the views of others, and not be rigid in his or her approach to problems.
5. Have a reasoned and balanced commitment to the social responsibilities of the corporation.
6. Have the interest and time available to be involved with the company and its employees over a sustained period.
7. Have the stature to represent the company before the public, its shareholders, and the other individuals and groups that affect the company.
8. Have a willingness to appraise management performance objectively, in the interest of all shareholders.

9. Have an open mind on the policy issues and areas of activity that affect the company and its shareholders.

10. And finally, not be involved in other activities or interests that conflict with his or her fiduciary responsibilities to the company and its shareholders.

We feel that we've been fortunate in finding people who meet these high standards for our board. And, once they are on our board, we work hard to help these talented individuals serve the company in every way possible.

How directors are chosen. A CEO should know a lot about a person before recommending him or her to the board. A common misconception is that the CEO chooses his or her golf partners. That's not always bad. But a systematic search procedure is more effective. Search firms can be important. They force attention to the desired criteria for your directors. They ensure that you're aware of many good candidates. They also can help you avoid individuals who would be a poor fit on the board.

Retirement age for directors. 72 is appropriate. For the most part, terms should start while a director is actively employed. When directors retire from their own companies, or change their primary occupation, their membership on the board should be reviewed. A question that must be asked: "Is this director still the best person to fill that slot?" This review should be a formal one, reported by the Nominating Committee to the full board.

Overall, this system of choosing and using directors has worked well at companies with which I'm familiar. Certainly, it's not perfect. But quite frankly, I'm not aware of any other system that works better.

All the support our directors gave us helped management not only weather its crises, but rebuild the company to industry leadership in six years. One incident stands out in particular— a takeover challenge. Our first response was to negotiate. But finally, we decided that the only thing left to do was to fight. The board was 100 percent behind that decision.

Particularly Arthur Granard, an Englishman who had planned the Allied air raids on Hitler's oil fields in Romania during World War II. When I called him to tell him we were going to fight the takeover, and to enlist his support, I remember him saying: "James, thank God you've finally come to that conclusion!" That's the kind of reaction a CEO really loves to hear!

I'm sure the prevailing system of corporate governance will continue to develop and change, as the issues and demands facing the modern corporation change.

But such changes can be evolutionary and dedicated to the long-term success of the corporation as a whole—as they must be, if free enterprise is to continue to work the economic miracles of which it is capable.

Communicating with key publics

A strong Board of Directors is the heart of a governance and accountability system—but it is not enough by itself. A corporation must maintain strong, effective, two-way communications with the much larger constituencies to whom it is accountable—employees, shareholders, government and political leaders, consumers and the general public. The support of all these groups is vital to the company's success, and you can't expect to get that support without asking for it and earning it.

Start with employees. They are not to be treated like mushrooms—told nothing, kept in the dark, and fed a load of manure at regular intervals. Employees should be treated more like sunflowers, which can reach great heights only if they bask in the sunlight of good communications.

Through the employee relations function, employees should be advised about the company's operations and strategies, its benefit plans, retirement options, job opportunities, savings options, promotions, and working conditions. Employees dedicate their working lives to the company; they are owed this attention. Beyond that, they will work more productively when they feel well-informed, when they know how their job relates to the company's overall health, and when they know that management really cares about their welfare.

True enough, there is no longer cradle-to-grave job security in any corporation, and the advent of advanced information technology has facilitated flatter organizational structures that require fewer managers and fewer total employees. But a knowledgeable workforce that has been treated like co-workers who are entitled to know the truth will outperform a worried, isolated workforce every time.

Similarly, a corporation's government relations effort must remain a priority both in good times and in bad—particularly for a multinational company in a highly visible field like the oil business. Operating in over 150 countries around the world, we found it well to stay out of politics and to concentrate on running the business, while keeping all governmental bodies well informed as to our environmental impact, taxation, workforce policies and supply availability (among many other things). In dealing with government especially, we found it far easier to make acquaintances and to establish lines of communication before they were needed than it was to look for such relationships when a crisis was already upon us.

Dealing with shareholder relations is another area of rapid change. Gone are the days when all a company had to publish was its street address and a very short annual statement. With modern electronic communications, with large institutional shareholders, with Internet trading, and with exchanges open somewhere in the world on a 24-hour basis, the investor relations function has become yet another challenge to management.

Some companies try to over-manage investor relations by, for example, forecasting earnings for analysts. But those turn into "analysts' expectations," which then become the business equivalent of the point spread in sports. The issue isn't, "did you win or lose?"—in other words, what did you earn for your shareholders? It becomes, "did you beat the point spread?" Did you meet the "whisper number," or some other supposedly accurate estimate of this quarter's earnings? That's a game you can't win.

There is, instead, a simple "miracle combination" for dealing with Wall Street. First you need a well-informed investor relations arm, which provides sufficient financial, operational and industry data to analysts to allow them to come to their own conclusions about the company. And then you need to earn a reputation for credibility.

Boards of directors don't like surprises; analysts and investors like them even less. Thus, making well-informed investor relations professionals always available to take a phone call creates a reputation for accessibility. And answering that phone call with straight-from-the-shoulder facts when there are some (and with a polite "I don't know" when necessary) forms the basis of a reputation for credibility.

Pre-emptive action can also be useful. At the time of the invasion of Kuwait by Iraq, for example, we held special meetings with analysts and with representatives of the press to explain the situation facing our facilities and to outline the petroleum supply flexibility in the industry. This action, and similar action by other companies, went a long way toward preventing consumer and shareholder panic. Similarly, the investment firms offered reassurance in the market corrections of 1987 and 1998, and the electronics industry suppliers explained the rapid decline in demand growth associated with the so-called "Asian Flu" in 1998-99.

Because of the rapidly changing nature and scope of investor relations activity, we welcomed the opportunity in 1993 to discuss that subject at the National Investor Relations Conference in New York City.

MILEPOST: NOVEMBER 5, 1992

Investor Relations' Role in a Successful Corporation

National Investor Relations Conference, New York

───────────

Good investor relations is absolutely essential to the success of a corporation. I once helped the Harvard Business School write a 40-page case study on Texaco. One of the points I made was the importance of good investor relations—to know who your constituencies are, and to work with them before you need them.

I have seen this situation demonstrated in other companies with which I am familiar. It is clear that investor relations is important in any corporation, and particularly in the oil business because of its very high public profile. Texaco's corporate logo stands at the corner of Elm and Main in virtually every city and town in the United States, and at highway interchanges all over the world. Everything we do, from drilling for oil to pumping gasoline, is subject to close public scrutiny. As far as I know gasoline is the only commodity in the United States where, by law, you have to have a price sign six inches high on the top of every pump—so we do get an awful lot of public scrutiny.

Part of that public consists of shareholders. We compete for investors just as we compete for customers at the pump. So in one sense, the shareholders vote on our performance every day in the stock market. We rank investor relations very high in our priority of things to do. It is key in our communications with the outside world. So I thought I'd try to give you some insight into the way our vice president for investor relations and I work together—and we do in fact work together—to make IR effective.

We could liken investor relations to an open window. Like any open window, things flow in both directions, both in and out. Outward, we try to build the company's reputation with the public. Inward, we get valuable intelligence about our industry, our competition, the marketplace and society. So let's talk first about the outward flow of information.

The starting point is our belief—and it's certainly my own very strongly held belief—that the reputation of a company is one of the four very vital factors that determine its stock price. The factors I look at are earnings per share, cash flow per share, dividends per share and corporate reputation. A company's reputation demands the most constant attention from senior management. Believe me, it can be very easy to damage a reputation. And it can be very hard to repair!

Reputation is very complex. It consists of the tangibles: How well do you do at finding oil? What percent of capacity are your refineries running at? And all that sort of thing. It also comprises intangible factors such as: What kind of corporate citizen are you? What are your people like? How do you manage your business? And, perhaps most importantly, how credible are you? It is hard to overstate the importance of credibility to a corporation, but there is no question in my mind that a good reputation for credibility can bring you an extra multiple in your price/earnings ratio.

> **A proxy fight is one of the ultimate tests of investor relations; not only to have a proxy fight and to do well, but to be alive and well thereafter.**

The value of credibility was demonstrated very clearly in 1988 during a very tough proxy fight with a well-known corporate raider. You may remember it. A proxy fight is one of the ultimate tests of investor relations; not only to have a proxy fight and to do well, but to be alive and well thereafter. That, in itself, is somewhat rare. But, if you've built your investor relations program on a solid basis of good performance and candid communications, then you've got the artillery you need.

We had that artillery in 1988. We had built our contacts with our investors before and during the litigation and ensuing bankruptcy, and I personally talked to every investor in the world with over about 20,000 shares. In a constant stream of personal meetings and other communications, we told them what we were up to and we listened to their concerns. They wanted to know our answer to their question, "This is fine, but what is your restructuring plan going to look like when you get out of this situation?"

As a result of all this contact, the shareholders knew us and they trusted us. That was good, because the proxy fight turned out to be quite a donnybrook. We fought share-by-share. Other members of senior management and I went out and met shareholders one-on-one and in groups throughout the country and literally around the world. We went to 21 cities in 15 days and we talked to every shareholder in those cities who wanted to talk to us. We reached thousands of others by mail and by telephone. And our theme was then, as it is today, "we do what we say we're going to do." We made the case and the hard work paid off. The shareholders voted overwhelmingly for management and the shareholders have turned out to be the winners. That's obviously why we did this.

The shareholders have done very well. Over the past five years, we have had a compound annual growth rate in annual total return to the shareholder of about 20 percent, a total of 139 percent. Since that time, we have stepped up our efforts to tell our story and we've had a very active investor relations program. I meet personally with large investors. We talk to all of them on the phone and respond quickly to their letters.

Now this doesn't mean, nor can it mean, that management does everything the stockholder wants management to do. You know, buying a share of stock is not like buying the local drug store. There are times, in fact every day, when we have to balance the long-term success of a corporation, as we see it, with the short-term desire of stockholders for ever-increased payout.

Management has to consider other constituencies as well. Certainly our shareholders are our prime constituency. But let's face it, we have employees, customers, people living in the communities where we operate, government officials, and regulators. We have to take note of all of them. If you've got a good investor relations program, backed by a reputation for credibility, you can explain to the shareholders your reasons for doing things and they will understand. If they feel comfortable with what management is telling them when times are good, then they will stick with you if times aren't so good. They are more likely, if they believe your story and believe in your credibility, to support your company on the important issues.

I believe this is a new era of investor relations. It's going to be more important in the future than it has been in the past. Discussion of litigation, environment, public policy, and government regulation are areas where I believe an informed shareholder public can be one of the most useful constituencies that we have. I have talked about this with the very large state pension funds, for example. I have written about it. These are the areas in which the investors are very interested.

We've taken the lead in alerting the public to the danger of excessive government regulation and—obviously in our business —ineffective regulations and unreasonable litigation. We've been talking about the cost-effective implementation of the Clean Air Act regulations that are very important in the oil industry. In this effort, our shareholders and employees have been important constituencies.

But in the long run, keeping your IR program effective depends most on maintaining credibility as a straight shooter. To build this credibility, the IR professional needs the full and enthusiastic backup of top management. If you haven't got it, you'd better get it, because that is what makes the program work. Unless management supports IR and shares its commitment to credibility and open access, the IR program cannot be successful. When our present management team took over six years ago, the analysts told us they weren't getting the full story on the company. That's being polite. They were getting approximations and numbers that tended to obscure the real state of affairs. We ended that very quickly. We opened the tent and we let them in. We showed the analysts exactly how we were doing.

> **Unless management supports IR and shares its commitment to credibility and open access, the IR program cannot be successful.**

We've continued to build our relationships with the investment community. Once a year we have a day-long presentation for analysts at our headquarters in Harrison. We encourage the analysts to attend, and we answer any questions they have for as long as they want to stay. We use the same charts and presentations we show to our board about the health of the company. And we make sure that our senior managers are there too, so they can mix with the analysts at the social hour and coffee breaks and answer their questions. That's a major change, and I think it's different from other companies. It used to be that you didn't allow the managers to attend because they might say something wrong to an analyst. No more! We're proud of our managers and we're proud of our plans.

In addition, top management travels around the country several times a year, meeting with analysts. We also go to Europe on a regular basis. There's a lot of money, and a lot of interested shareholders, in London, Edinburgh, Zurich and Paris—and we try to visit them all. Investor Relations plays a big part in planning for all these events.

We try to be as accessible as possible to the press—the business press and the general press. We stress a few key themes. It's better to get the message across to the public on the major points, rather than try to cover the waterfront. Whenever we have a meeting with the press or go on television, we try to get out just a few major themes or ideas.

Like many companies, we have an array of effective investor relations tools to help us. Some of our publications, such as the Annual Report, are geared for the general investor. Each Annual Report has a theme and it will tell a good story about the company. We also have other more sophisticated publications, like the Statistical Supplement, which are targeted for the analysts and the professional investor.

> **Our investor relations function gives us a good "ear to the ground" on Wall Street.**

Several years ago, analysts and investors told us they wanted to hear more about our strategies and not so much about our results. They said: "Tell us how the next five years are going to look." Of course, we can't do that because we don't know, but we can show them what our plans are. We did that. And I'm happy to say our Annual Report recently won a major award from the International Association of Business Communicators for its clear and candid explanation of our business strategies.

Articulating our strategies in public has been a valuable experience for us, too. We found that having to explain them to others encourages sound, realistic planning. It also imposes a certain amount of discipline on a corporation. If you say what you're going to do, and you put your plan out in public, then you had better go out and do it.

Communications flow both ways. I've been talking about the flow outward. Let's think about the flow inward. By gathering intelligence from outside sources, a good investor relations program can sensitize management to things that are going on out there. Changes, for example, in accounting policy. I know during the time I handled investor relations, I became sensitized to issues such as full cost accounting, equity accounting and share buy-backs—areas that I had never devoted any time or thought to. But I started to study them and I learned a lot. It helps our management anticipate social trends and legislation, including accounting changes and market shifts that can affect our business. I have no doubt that these broader social and political issues will continue to show up in more and more of the proxy statements of American companies, so it makes a lot of sense to have the shareholders in your corner.

Our investor relations function also gives us a good "ear to the ground" on Wall Street. It helps us figure out how the market is going to interpret or react to announcements, so we can position any announcements we have to be most effective.

Security analysts tell us what the competition is up to. And one of the hallmarks we stress today is paying attention to what the competition is doing. We are a very competitively driven company and we get an enormous amount of very valuable, competitive information by reading the reports we get from the analysts. It helps us to measure our own performance against that of the competition.

In one sense, you can say that analyst reports are our report card. The analysts rate our performance and they provide insight into where we can do better. We make these reports available to our board—not only available, but we send them out, warts and all. We don't cull the good reports from the bad. We send them all, good and bad. The directors are always looking for ways to measure management's performance. So if the reports are favorable (as I'm happy to tell you they have been in recent years), it builds the board's confidence in management. It makes them receptive to the ideas of management.

We've done something else recently which I think is innovative and good. We have spelled out in black and white our board's requirements and expectations of executive management. We set down what is expected of management by the board and in a parallel column what is expected of the board by management. I think this is a very important document because it shows we are obviously moving into a new world of increased sensitivity in corporate governance. On both sides there is a need for full, open and honest communication with the public. Our Investor Relations program helps us to meet that need. It is highly valued and is shaped by our Board of Directors.

Good investor relations also have to be based on an understanding that both shareholders and security analysts have changed in recent years. When I first started doing IR, there were something like 7,500 analysts. There aren't so many now because, as you know, the balance of shareholders has shifted to the larger investors. Individuals are proportionately a small part of the mix for most corporations. In one sense, that's too bad, because the smaller shareholders tend to hold shares longer and identify personally with the company. And certainly, they favor our products and our services and credit cards.

We try to encourage individual investments, whether by employees, our credit-card holders or the general public. One way we do this is to make it easy for our investors to buy shares directly, and we have such a program. But I expect the trend to continue in the other direction, with more and more shareholdings being made by the larger investors. They tend to be more knowledgeable, more sophisticated and more demanding of information.

Since 1987, the number of analysts covering the industry has dropped. There is not as much hard research being done on the sell side on Wall Street. Each analyst has to cover more companies than he or she has in the past. Thus, it is important for investor relations professionals to understand what information the analysts and the large investors need. Because they are covering more companies, they need that information more quickly, and it is up to us to provide it to them. So it's more work for us. But it is also a great opportunity for IR people. It means you must make sure the analysts get the full story you want to tell them. You can stress the themes that are important to your management and make the case that you want to make.

With companies depending more and more on investor relations, the demands on IR professionals are going to grow. How can you best prepare yourself for this challenge? My advice would be to learn everything you can about your company, your industry and how you operate. To communicate what your company is doing, you have to understand its operations. You have to understand finance and the marketplace. And I think it is very important for IR people to cultivate operating people, financial types and marketers. Our IR vice president has literally traveled around the world looking at Texaco's operations. She's been to the Partitioned Neutral Zone in the Middle East, to Saudi Arabia, and to Europe. She has seen and met and talked, firsthand, to operators in the fields and the oil ministers in their offices. Believe me, that gives her credibility—that word again!—credibility when she talks to the shareholders. So try to do that, to get out of the office and talk to the people on the assembly line and on the floor of the warehouse.

There is also at least a dose of communications and salesmanship in investor relations as well. The most effective IR professionals can relate to investors and to analysts, and understand their needs. The numbers are important, but so are people skills.

Finally, to meet the challenges ahead, I urge you to work to find new ways to be indispensable to your company's management. The definition of investor relations is not always set in stone. The more ways you can find to be valuable to your management, the more effective you can be.

So in sum, what are the key points in an effective investor relations program? First, basic credibility. Second, the full and enthusiastic backing of your top management. Third, IR professionals who understand the business and the business community.

In my view, only the very best companies will survive and prosper in the tough global marketplace that is obviously now emerging. But, with these three tools—credibility, backing of top management and an understanding of your business and the investment community—you can make a major impact on the ability of your company to compete in that marketplace.

6

Oil and
International Relations

O ver the past century, oil supplies have strongly influenced military power and diplomacy. Wars have been fought over oil. Access to petroleum has fueled the success of the victors, while shortage of fuel has contributed to the demise of the losers. In our time we see this pattern of conflicts over oil most clearly in the Middle East—though the military and foreign-policy impact of petroleum has not been confined to that region, and petroleum has not been the only source of conflict in the Middle East.

Ever since the separation of the sons of Abraham into the ancient tribes of Ishmael and Isaac, in fact, there have been tensions, strife and warfare in what we now call the Middle East. Boundaries in this vast area of sand, mountains, deserts of searing heat, and fertile valleys and coastal plains have moved with the rise and fall of empires and with the success or failure of their armies. In modern periods, the Western powers imposed their own sense of equity on the region through a series of protectorates, treaties and, lately, United Nations resolutions.

Other divisions are religious in nature. The Moslem nations are split among the more liberal Sunni and the more fundamentalist Shiite sects; to this day, the Iranian Shiite radio transmitters bombard the largely Sunni population across the Gulf with their own brand of fundamentalist hate mail. The mutual distrust between Israel and most of the Arab world is well known, also.

But the discovery of oil in the southern Persian (or Arabian) Gulf gave a new dimension to all these conflicts. There arose natural jealousies between sparsely populated states that were rich in oil—Saudi Arabia, Iraq, Kuwait and the United Arab Emirates—and those less favored in geology, such as Lebanon, Syria, Jordan and Egypt. And oil gave the outside world a much larger stake in the affairs of the Middle East.

Since the Second World War ended, the region has seen a seemingly endless string of crises—armed conflict over the nationalization of the Suez Canal in 1956, the Six-Day War between Israel and the Arab states in 1967, the Arab oil embargo of 1973, and the Iranian revolution in 1979. Between 1980 and 1988 Iraq and Iran fought a devastating war over (among other things) access to the deep water at Shatt-al-Arab, where the legendary Tigris-Euphrates river system flows into the Gulf. Then came Iraq's occupation of Kuwait and the Gulf War of 1990-91.

Such a history of conflict in any region would have had a troubling impact on the rest of the world. But the importance of oil to the world economy has made the conflicts in the Middle East all the more important. Each of these crises in the Middle East has created a panic in world oil markets, due to real or perceived shortages of crude oil and/or tanker capacity.

After the long and ruinous war with Iran in the 1980s, the Iraqis needed both additional oil revenue and a military success for their own internal purposes. Saddam Hussein, their long-time leader, cast a covetous eye to the south on Kuwait, which he referred to as the long-lost 13th province of Iraq. The Emirate of Kuwait, though only about the size of Los Angeles County, contained proven reserves of 100 billion barrels of oil, and produced over 3 million barrels per day. With only a small population and no natural barriers along the border, Kuwait looked like an easy target.

South of Kuwait, between Kuwait City and Saudi Arabia, lies the Partitioned Neutral Zone, created in 1922 to settle border disputes between Kuwait and Saudi Arabia. The zone is defined by the Saudis' most northerly boundary claim, the Kuwaitis' most southerly claim, and the Gulf to the east. The surface area of the northern half of the PNZ is administered by the Kuwaitis, the southern half by the Saudis;

but the rights to underground mineral resources throughout the Zone are held in undivided joint interest by the two countries.

In 1949, with some encouragement from the U.S. government, John Paul Getty had obtained an exploration and production concession from the Saudis covering their on-shore interests in the PNZ. A subsequent exploration program discovered the Wafra and South Um Ghadir fields. The operation became the property of Texaco in 1984 with its acquisition of Getty.

These fields are not large by Mideast standards, but eventually were developed with an estimate of at least a billion barrels of recoverable reserves. The fields have relatively low pressure, and thus for the most part are produced by 800 pumping wells that were extracting 140,000 barrels per day in 1990. The operation included a small, simple refinery on the coast, with an office building and a housing area nearby. The Kuwaitis refer to the area as Mina al-Zour; the Saudis call it Mina al-Saud.

Further to the southeast of the PNZ lie Saudi Arabia, with its tremendous producing capacity of over 10 million barrels per day, and Bahrain—which has minimal production now but has an important place in world petroleum history.

It was in Bahrain in 1932 that the Standard Oil Company of California, operating without today's sophisticated exploratory tools, drilled on a surface anticline, discovered oil and developed a well producing 10,000 barrels per day—the first production in the southern part of the Gulf. This success led to the partnership between Standard Oil of California (later Chevron) and Texaco, who together founded several successful corporations—including the Bahrain Petroleum Company, the Arabian-American Oil Company, Caltex Petroleum Corporation, and Caltex Pacific Indonesia.

Only 50 miles across an arm of the Arabian Gulf from Bahrain, the venture's geologists found another surface anticline, this one at Dammam, Saudi Arabia. After six unsuccessful wells, Dammam #7 found oil in 1938. From this modest beginning grew Aramco, presently the world's largest oil producer. Exxon and Mobil bought in as additional owners of Aramco in 1945.

In the fall of 1964, as a member of the Aramco Study Group representing Texaco's interest in Aramco, I made my first of many trips to Saudi Arabia. It was a kingdom in a region of mystery and ancient history, as well as the world's fastest growing major oil producer. At that time it was producing more than 1.6 million barrels of oil per day—which was enormous production at the time, but only one-sixth of today's Saudi capacity of 10 million barrels per day.

Our group stayed in the Aramco camp in Dhahran, which looked very much like a new suburb in Southern California. Over 2,000 expatriates (mostly Americans) lived in Dhahran with their families. Very few Saudis were even close to attaining senior management positions at that time.

We took a small plane some 400 miles to the Rub'al-Khali, or "Empty Quarter," in the southeastern part of the country. There, in mountains of reddish-brown sand and sparse vegetation, was a lonely party of seismic explorationists. The temperature was over 130 degrees and the only air conditioning was in the explorationists' truck (where we could spend very little time, unfortunately). That crew and its truck were the forebears of the Shaybah Field, brought on stream in 1998. The field produces over 500,000 barrels per day of Arabian Extra Light crude oil. The sand mountains with their long patterns of light against dark shadows are still there, and the light, sweet crude oil is as environmentally benign as crude oil can be.

Shaybah is but one of many miracles in the desert. Another, more fundamental one in which we can take pride is the transfer of technology that has occurred over the years. Today I am still privileged to visit the Dhahran camp, and it still looks like a Southern California suburb—but the managers are virtually all Saudis.

By July of 1990, when the crisis over Kuwait began, Aramco was producing over 7 million barrels per day, and had the capacity to produce much more.

Kuwait and the PNZ, then, were the prizes that caused the gleam in the eyes of Saddam Hussein as his forces, led by the Republican Guard, swept south from Iraq on August 2, 1990, overwhelming Kuwait and the Partitioned Neutral Zone and stopping only at the Saudi border.

For the remainder of 1990, the U.S. and other nations tried through diplomatic means to remove the Iraqi forces from Kuwait. A peaceful solution was not found. But the U.S. was successful in putting together a coalition of countries to stand with it as more forceful actions were planned.

Most of Texaco's employees at Mina al-Saud had been forced to evacuate on August 2. The company manager was the last to leave, on a tugboat at midnight (though the chief accountant sneaked back through enemy lines several days later to retrieve computer tapes of the operation—such is the nature of chief accountants!).

The Iraqis used the company's headquarters and administrative office building as a command post, with a machine-gun nest on the roof and bunkers for the troops throughout the camp. The beaches were covered with barbed wire to repel an invasion from the sea (rumors of which had been reported on CNN).

Meanwhile the Texaco refinery had been reduced to the appearance of a bowl of black spaghetti, and the housing areas were looted and burned. The surface casing of each of the producing wells had been circled with TNT, which was then detonated; the pumping units landed hundreds of yards away. The entire producing field was also planted by the Iraqis with over a million land mines. (Even after liberation, children, camels and sheep in particular were the unfortunate victims of these subsurface explosives, because they did not and could not know to keep to the pathways that had been swept clear of mines.)

On January 17, 1991, U.S. Apache aircraft opened fire on the Iraqi forces, and an all-out attack by U.S. Air Force, Navy and allied aircraft began, striking at targets from Baghdad to the Saudi Arabian border. On February 24, a ground attack began sweeping west and north to surround the Iraqi forces. There was a furious four-day fight, but on February 28 a cease-fire took effect. Iraqi forces were out of Kuwait and out of the PNZ. And although the oil fields were still on fire, the rebuilding was about to begin.

Texaco employees in the Zone, who numbered almost 900, had been dispersed throughout Saudi Arabia. But starting on March 6, 1991—with added professionals in the fields of firefighting, bomb disposal, demolition and construction—they were back on the job. By October 1991 the last oil fire was extinguished, and by the end of the year the last flowing well was capped.

Oil began to be produced again on March 1, 1992, and soon production reached 80,000 barrels per day. The Saudi and the Kuwaiti oil ministers accepted Texaco's invitation to take part in a ceremony held on March 3, 1992, marking the resumption of production in the Zone.

Hundreds of employees, dependents, government officials and news media reporters were on hand. For the occasion large tents, Oriental carpets, gold-painted chairs, a magnificent buffet, and a rising stem valve on a simulated pipeline were provided.

Like the setting, the speech I gave was somewhat exotic—and both are illustrative of the challenges that American executives will increasingly face communicating in lands, in languages and with cultures far different from our own.

I had little to do with writing the actual text of this speech. It was composed in Arabic, by a colleague of Egyptian birth who was skilled as a writer, a veteran of the oil industry, and knowledgeable about both Western and Arabic culture. The speech was translated into English for my delivery. But it was the Arabic version that was key for our audiences, which is why it was written in Arabic to begin with. Simultaneous interpretation was provided at the event, because most of the 400 people in attendance were more fluent in Arabic than in English.

The formal, almost flowery language may sound strange to our ears. But it was essential in conveying the tone of mutual respect and mutual commitment that I needed to communicate to these people who were so important to our business. And the message carried far beyond that tent in the desert; indeed, the Arabic version was printed in its entirety in virtually every newspaper in the Middle East. A valve-turning picture made most of the television news programs in the region—and, from the Saudi point of view, reinforced the idea that having a strong American partner was a strategic advantage.

MILEPOST: MARCH 3, 1992

Saudi Arabia: A Special Relationship

Ceremony Marking Resumption of Production, Partitioned Neutral Zone

---

Al Salaam Aleikum. Peace be with you.

For over half a century the Kingdom of Saudi Arabia and Texaco have cooperated within a special relationship that has been based on mutual esteem and common interests.

These decades have witnessed many a wonder—from the early days of the Dammam Dome* to the considerable accomplishments of Star Enterprise. In that time, we have developed a partnership in a variety of joint projects, which has been unique in the annals of the oil industry.

We all know how vast and parched is this ancient land and how harsh and difficult are the natural and climatic conditions in Arabia.

That is all the more reason for the Saudi people and their leaders to feel justly proud at having accomplished so many of their extraordinary dreams and of making them into ordinary reality through the successful achievements of the five-year plans, whose scope and speed of development have been truly spectacular.

Much of the credit goes to the sagacity of the Saudi rulers who, like skilled navigators, cautiously guided their state through the turbulent waters of change by encouraging all the modern and technical innovations within the established equilibrium provided by the maintenance of traditional cultural and social frameworks.

At every stage of this period, Texaco, as a technologically advanced energy enterprise, cooperated with the Kingdom in many areas.

---

* *In 1938 Texaco and Chevron drilled the discovery well Dammam #7 on the Dammam Dome. This represented the first commercial discovery of oil in Saudi Arabia (after six unsuccessful wells), and marked the first chapter in the long history of Saudi Aramco.*

Both parties worked on a ground of understanding that is based on that most uncommon thing called common sense.

That went a long way toward the practical solution of problems in an amicable way for our mutual advantage.

I am personally pleased to say that I have been, over these many years, both a participant and an initiator in many chapters of this successful story. From my first encounter with the Saudis, I have experienced the courtesy and hospitality, which is their inherited tradition and way of life.

In our daily dealings with Saudi officials, we have endeavored to promote and maintain constructive, effective and friendly relations.

I would like particularly to salute His Excellency, Hisham Nazer, who is one of those fortunate leaders whose fine talent has been singularly suited to the challenges of his demanding and successful career, and who has played such a helpful role in solidifying the collaborative efforts between the Kingdom and the company.

It is fortunate that, in the joint operations, we have the cooperation of the two countries, Saudi Arabia and Kuwait, whose close relations are built on shared family ties, common cultural heritage, and unity of objectives.

Their development and administration of the Zone constitute an exemplary instance of fruitful cooperation among neighboring nations who have conducted their relations on the basis of international legitimacy and reciprocal interests.

In expressing our deep appreciation to His Excellency, Dr. Humoud Abdellah Al-Rqobah, for his kindly collaboration, we voice our admiration for the way he faced the tide of troubles and distressing deeds.

The bravery and ingenuity of the engineers and workers under his direction allowed the fires to be extinguished and production to be restored well ahead of the time anyone had originally anticipated.

We hope that the liberation and restoration of legitimacy will bring peace, order and stability.

In the Koran, it is written that if God had willed it, he could have made us all one nation—but instead he has created us of different nations and backgrounds so that, when acquainted, each would bring his special contribution to a common cause.

In our joint enterprises, the company has relied on employees and representatives who are Saudi, Kuwaiti, American and of other nationalities, all participating together, in spite of cultural diversity, to fulfill the main aim, which is to move forward in achieving the mutual benefits of progress and prosperity.

Saudi Arabia has by far the greatest potential of any nation to help meet the world's energy demands. Texaco, as a great international oil organization, will continue to cooperate and contribute its varied technical capacities and skills.

Events sometimes make it seem as if life is a continuum, consisting of a series of confusions and calamities, as all of us, separately and together, have experienced disheartening trials and tribulations, which required stoical strength and stamina to surmount.

I especially would like to mention, with appreciation, Saudi support and sympathy which we experienced during our company's recent times of trouble, when so many foreboding clouds hovered over us.

With optimism and goodwill, we shall continue on our course of cooperation, which has been beneficial for all sides, sustained by the belief that our universe is infused by the Almighty with pattern and purpose, and sharing also that brightly burning spirit of free enterprise which feels that no problem is too difficult to face and no obstacle too great to overcome.

Encouraged by what has been accomplished so far, and strengthened by adversity, which has brought out the best in us, it is easier to see why we embark on this latest of enterprises with confidence, and why we foresee the future cooperation among the Kingdom of Saudi Arabia, Kuwait and Texaco as full of hope and promise.

The historical backdrop

The Gulf War may loom large in our memories today, but it is just one illustration of how important oil supply has been to diplomacy and to military power for nearly 100 years.

In the late 19th and early 20th centuries the British Navy depended on a worldwide network of coaling stations from Gibraltar to the Falklands, Samoa, Trincomalee, Aden and Suez. When oil replaced coal as the fuel in the warships of the world in the first part of the 20th Century, dependability of worldwide supply was a great strategic advantage, first for the British and increasingly for the United States.

The availability of usable petroleum products depends upon access to crude supplies, refining capacity, strategically located terminals, and tanker capacity to link them all together. Each of these elements of petroleum supply has been the target of concentrated attack in wartime. The RAF's bombing of the oilfields and refineries of Ploesti in Romania in 1944, and the German U-boat attacks on the Allied Atlantic tanker fleet, were efforts to deny fuel to the enemy. The U.S. Navy's submarine force in the Pacific inflicted mortal damage on Japan's supply lines from Indonesia to the home islands.

The denial of oil supplies to the enemy by the Allied forces eventually played a large role in the defeat of Germany and of Japan. And in each of the military actions since then—from Korea in 1950, to Vietnam in 1960, to the Gulf War in 1990—petroleum supply to the military has been a major consideration for every combatant. Even in the limited conflict of the Gulf War, the needs were enormous; the industry was asked by the Saudi Government to assist in the supply of 500,000 barrels per day of aviation fuel for the coalition aircraft.

This interrelationship between petroleum supply and military preparedness has long been understood to be such an important issue that it receives major attention in the studies at the U.S. Naval War College in Newport, Rhode Island, where officers from the U.S. and other NATO forces undergo rigorous training in strategy and tactics. At the suggestion of the retired Chairman of the Joint Chiefs of Staff, Admiral William J. Crowe, I was invited to address these issues by taking part in the Contemporary Civilization Lecture Series at the U.S. Naval War College. This invitation presented a unique opportunity to record some historical aspects of military fuel supply, and also to suggest some considerations for the future.

MILEPOST: FEBRUARY 9, 1993

Oil and the Military: The Challenge of Leadership

U.S. Naval War College, Newport, Rhode Island

The United States Navy and the oil business have been intimately connected throughout this century, ever since oil began to fuel the industrial might that is the basis of America's role as a world power.

And it is no coincidence, in my view, that this hundred-year period of history has been called both "The American Century" and "The Century of Oil."

The latter is the name given to it by the author, Daniel Yergin. I hope you were able to see the recent series on public television, based on Mr. Yergin's book about oil, *The Prize*. It was fascinating.

In that book, he calls petroleum "the motive force of industrial society and the lifeblood of the civilization it helped create."

Now the 20th Century is marching toward its conclusion. And there are some who have questioned whether American power, and the role of oil in our civilization, might not be waning as well.

I have some strong convictions on those points. And that's what I'd like to share with you tonight.

It's hard to imagine what today's world would be like without oil. And it's even more striking to consider just how rapidly oil became the lifeblood of modern civilization.

The first oil well was drilled in 1859, in Pennsylvania. At first, oil's primary use was to make kerosene for lamps. But by the beginning of this century, oil was beginning to be used as a powerful new fuel. And it was changing the world.

Oil powered the early motor vehicles of Daimler in Germany and Ford in America. It lifted the Wright Brothers off the sands at Kitty Hawk. And it would inspire the most profound changes in warfare since the invention of gunpowder.

In 1911, at the instigation of the young First Lord of the Admiralty, Winston Churchill, the Royal Navy switched from coal to oil, to power the ships that held together the British Empire.

Oil also made possible another military innovation championed by Churchill, the tank. Soon, the tank would make trench warfare obsolete. And along with the airplane, it would turn "blitzkrieg" into a household word a generation later.

In the Second World War the outcome, in both Europe and the Pacific, was determined in part by oil.

In 1940, in the Battle of Britain, Spitfires were fueled with 100-octane aviation fuel, which had been developed in the U.S. and The Netherlands during the 1930s. This provided the vital performance edge they needed to defeat the Nazi Messerschmitt 109s, which ran on 87-octane gasoline.

In 1941, Hitler ignored his generals' advice to take Moscow. Instead, he turned his troops south, lured by the oil fields of Baku, in the southern Soviet Union, only to have them run out of fuel before they could get there.

The allies exploited Germany's vulnerability in oil. In 1944, two days after the Normandy invasion, U.S. General Carl Spaatz directed that "The primary strategic aim of the United States strategic air forces is now to deny oil to enemy armed forces."

Germany's synthetic oil production facilities and its Romanian oil fields at Ploesti were prime targets of allied bombers.

Oil was also central to the Pacific war. Japan had counted on using oil from conquered areas of Malaysia and Indonesia to fuel its war machine. They even produced oil from one of our Texaco fields in Sumatra, where we're still pumping today. But U.S. submarines cut their tanker lifeline, hastening Japan's defeat.

One of the more heroic incidents of the Second World War involved a Texaco tanker, the *S.S. Ohio*. In 1942, the British still held the Mediterranean island of Malta, between Italy and Tunisia, despite a ferocious Axis bombardment and blockade.

Malta was key. It was the Allies' only base in the area. From it, Allied aircraft could attack the Axis shipping that was supplying Rommel in North Africa.

Rommel, of course, was also driven by a thirst for oil. He was seeking to cut off the British lifeline at Suez, and then link up in the Caucasus with the German forces driving on the Soviet oil fields.

By August of '42, Malta was running out of aviation fuel and other supplies. So a convoy of Allied ships set out from England, through the Straits of Gibraltar, to resupply the island fortress. Among them was the Texaco tanker *Ohio*, the fastest tanker in the U.S. fleet.

The convoy was attacked by wave after wave of Axis dive-bombers and U-boats. The log of the Ohio for August 13 noted that bombs, falling on all sides, were all exceptionally near misses. But it felt as if they'd "lifted the vessel clean out of the water."

The ship was badly damaged, and 12 of its 23-man crew were killed. Nevertheless, the *Ohio* limped into Malta, delivering 12,000 tons of aviation fuel to the British. Resupplied, they continued to choke off Rommel's fuel supplies. Soon, he was driven out of Africa.

Last summer, 50 years after that heroic passage, Texaco representatives flew to Malta. They joined Her Majesty Queen Elizabeth in commemorating the event, paying homage to the *Ohio*. A few weeks later, the company launched its first double-hulled tanker, which was named the *Star Ohio*, after its gallant predecessor.

Texaco has continued to contribute significantly to U.S. military operations in the years since World War II. In Korea, I was a young ensign at the Inchon landing. I didn't know it at the time, but much of the fuel for the planes flying cover for our fleet came from Texaco.

My company also was the largest supplier of military fuel during the Vietnam War. And during "Operation Desert Storm," we helped provide coalition forces with the half-million barrels a day of aviation fuel they needed.

> **Throughout this century, America's oil industry has supported our national interests, in peacetime as in war.**

At one point in the Persian Gulf War, Texaco played a direct role in a moment of high drama. One of our managers had fled Kuwait, and was in Saudi Arabia. One night, the U.S. Central Command called him at 2 a.m.

The Iraqis had opened Kuwaiti valves, and oil was pouring into the Gulf. It was an environmental disaster. They needed advice on what to do, and they needed it fast.

Well, our Texaco manager was very familiar with the piping system. He told the military how they could cut off the flow, by bombing the manifold at a pumping station. The Kuwaitis pinpointed the exact location, and U.S. airpower did the rest. The flow was stopped.

We felt pretty good about helping out. But it was nothing new for us, or for other companies in our business. Throughout this century, America's oil industry has supported our national interests, in peacetime as in war.

America's great prosperity, which in recent years has spread to other nations, was built on abundant, reliable and affordable fuel. Today, fully 60 percent of U.S. energy comes from oil and natural gas, including 97 percent of its transportation fuel. The "American Way of Life" would not be possible without petroleum.

Yet, ironically, the public's view of oil and the oil industry remains, at best, a love-hate relationship. I'm no psychologist, but I suppose that's inevitable, when your enterprise is so central to people's lives that they depend on it.

A few years ago, there were plenty of pundits who were ready, and indeed eager, to write off the oil industry. Petroleum, they said, has seen its day. It was going the way of the buggy whip.

At the same time, many critics were eagerly writing the epitaph for America's role in the future, as well. The United States was a declining nation, they said. It would soon be replaced as a world leader by another power, or combination of powers.

Well, the events of the past few years—particularly in Iraq— have shown these predictions to be, at the very least, premature.

Both oil and American military power will continue to be essential for many years to come. They'll both continue to be desperately needed, greatly appreciated, and, in some cases, deeply resented, by the people of the world.

And because of this, I think there are a great many similarities between the challenges faced by the leaders of the military and those of the oil industry, now and in the years to come. Let me tell you what I mean.

For one thing, the men and women running both enterprises will have to operate in a world that's become far more complex and fast-moving than it used to be. They'll have to do their jobs under many more constraints than their predecessors ever faced.

They'll have to do them with even greater sensitivity to the environment. To local cultures, to rapidly changing demographics and lifestyles, and to the impact of their actions on the economy.

They'll have to do their jobs with fewer people and fewer dollars. Both the military and the oil industry have been going through periods of downsizing and cost cutting. And all indications are that this will continue.

Because of the growing premium on individual initiative, military and oil industry leaders also will have to develop the talents and enthusiasm of each employee to the fullest. But at the same time, they'll have to harness and coordinate those qualities for the benefit of the overall organization.

That's a big order. Doing all this will demand more effective leadership, more skill, and more wisdom than ever before.

With those parallels between oil and the military as background, let me briefly sketch for you some of the major issues we're facing in the oil industry today, and how we're dealing with them.

Fundamental is that, long-term, the demand for energy has been rising and will continue to rise in the years to come. In the United States, it's gone up by almost two percent a year since the beginning of the 1980s.

Our population keeps growing. People are driving more, and using more power-driven gadgets. The same thing is happening in Europe, Japan and the rest of the Pacific Rim. And it will doubtless happen, sooner or later, in Latin America, China, and the former communist world. And, of course, all that takes energy.

America's role in the global oil scene is declining.

World oil supplies are adequate for present needs. But America's role in the global oil scene is declining, in relative terms. And there are some serious consequences of this.

America has dominated the world of oil since the beginning. Today, the U.S. still has the biggest oil industry in the world. It is one of America's core industries.

Nevertheless, the domestic oil industry is shrinking, due to a number of reasons. Foremost are some destructive trends in public policy: over-regulation in general, runaway environmental regulation in particular, and the enormous cost of the attendant litigation.

Because of pressure from environmental special interests, much of the U.S. East and West coasts has been declared off-limits for oil production. So has the Arctic National Wildlife Reserve in Alaska, which contains the most promising large reserves in this country. This means we have to look for new oil mainly in other countries.

In 1991, U.S. crude oil production fell to its lowest level in three decades. We're now importing fully one-half of all the crude oil we use. And we expect imports to grow to 60 percent by the end of the decade.

For the first 11 months of 1992, the net cost of imported oil equaled 55 percent of the total U.S. trade deficit.

Oil refining, as well as production, is also declining in the U.S. In effect, we are exporting our refining industry. Due to costs and environmental opposition, no major oil refinery has been built in this country for more than a decade. Existing ones are downsizing or shutting down all around us.

All these trends raise the cost of fuel and energy for Americans. They siphon money and resources from other uses, such as rebuilding the infrastructure. And they affect national security.

They also cost American jobs. Both those in companies that move operations abroad because of high energy costs here at home. And in the oil industry itself.

Everyone's heard about the problems of the U.S. automobile industry. But few people realize that, while Detroit has lost 100,000 jobs in the last decade, the U.S. oil industry has lost 450,000 jobs, or 50 percent of the total.

In my view, the same uncertainties that will require us to maintain strong armed services will also require a secure, geographically diverse supply of energy to fuel a growing U.S. economy. Oil is fundamental to economic progress, and there is nothing on the horizon that can replace it economically.

> **It's unrealistic to think that the United States will ever be 100 percent energy sufficient.**

It's unrealistic to think that the United States will ever be 100 percent energy sufficient. But certainly, we can be more independent than we have been, while lowering our trade deficit and saving American jobs at the same time.

To rebuild our economy and create new jobs, and for national security as well, we need economic and tax policies that encourage the production of ample energy at affordable prices.

As I once told Admiral Crowe, either this country adopts an intelligent national energy policy, or we'd better start building some more aircraft carriers, to protect our lines of supply.

Over-regulation is one of the complex issues facing the oil industry. From time to time, various proposals surface to regulate the price of oil, gasoline or natural gas. That was tried back in the 1970s, and it was a disaster. It contributed to the fuel shortages of 1973 and 1979.

Oil prices were completely decontrolled in 1981. And energy markets have worked extremely well ever since. The U.S. consumer is well served by continued strong competition between suppliers.

The nationalization of the oil industries in other nations is also a matter of concern in my business. There has been a trend toward this since the early '70s.

With some ingenuity, we can deal with it, and even turn it to our advantage. Back in 1976, the Saudi Arabian government bought the rights and assets of Aramco, the Arabian-American Oil Company, within the Kingdom. Texaco had been part of Aramco, which produces all the oil in that country, and the action ended our concession there.

But a decade later, we struck an innovative deal with the Saudis that benefits both sides. We established a 50-50 venture called Star Enterprise, to operate all our refining and marketing operations in the eastern United States. Star sells products and services under the Texaco brand name.

The agreement gave Saudi Arabia access to the world's biggest gasoline market, and gave us access to 600,000 barrels a day of Saudi crude oil, at market prices, for 20 years. This ensures us a supply of consistently high-quality crude, well into the next century.

Setting up Star Enterprise was a new and innovative approach. But it was based on a very successful example: a 50-year-old marketing and manufacturing join venture called Caltex, which Texaco owns with Chevron. Caltex commands an 18 percent share of the gasoline market in the Pacific Rim.

Like N.A.T.O., Caltex and Star are examples of strategic alliances formed to help their members adapt to changing conditions.

In an uncertain future, the kind of ingenuity that led to the establishment of Star Enterprise will become even more vital for both the military and the oil industry.

A lot of that ingenuity can be found in the research laboratory. We're already using state-of-the-art technology that's almost as impressive as the wizardry that guided America's smart bombs down Saddam Hussein's chimneys.

To find new oil, we're using such advanced methods as satellite imaging and three-dimensional seismic technology. And we've got horizontal drilling, as well as steam, water and CO_2 injection, to produce more of the oil in the ground.

In refining, our scientists are developing new processes that allow us to produce more valuable, high-end products, such as gasoline and aviation fuel, from each barrel of oil.

Advanced technology, of course, is extremely expensive. For that reason, in these times of tight budgets and limited resources, I believe we're going to see a major expansion in partnerships to develop technology that has both military and civilian applications.

Certainly, there's plenty of precedent for this: radio communications; the jeep; civilian jet aircraft. I'm a director of Corning, and the famous Corning Ware cooking utensils are made of a material developed for rocket nose cones in the 1950s.

As valuable as leading-edge technology is, leadership is perhaps the greatest asset that any organization—military or industrial—has in dealing with the challenges facing it.

I'll always be grateful to the Navy for the leadership skills I learned. They've been invaluable throughout my career. Quite frankly, without my Navy experience, I don't think I'd be where I am today.

In conclusion, let me just say that I consider myself to be a very fortunate individual. For the past 40 years, I've been blessed to work in the oil business. I have found that experience to be as challenging, exciting and, ultimately, as much fun as anyone could want.

As Daniel Yergin wrote in *The Prize*, "No other business so starkly and extremely defines the meaning of risk and reward, and the profound impact of chance and fate," as does the oil industry.

I was also fortunate to get my education and start my career in the United States Navy. President Kennedy once said: "Any man who may be asked what he did to make his life worthwhile can respond with a good deal of pride and satisfaction, 'I served in the United States Navy.'"

As a Navy man and an oil man, I am confident that the leaders of these two great enterprises have the ability to meet whatever fate sends our way in the future.

■

The issue of sanctions

History has demonstrated how important it is to deny strategic goods to an enemy in time of war. This experience has tempted governmental leaders also to deny goods and trade to countries with whom we are engaged in conflicts that fall short of war. The use of economic sanctions as a tool of foreign policy has been a particular habit of the United States; in just the four years from 1993 through 1996, for example, the U.S imposed sanctions 61 times against 35 countries.

Sanctions have come in a variety of forms, always denying the sanctioned nation something of economic value that it otherwise would have enjoyed. They have involved trade, credit, travel, war materiel, foodstuffs, petroleum, capital, and payment of bills, among other things.

Because of its central position in world commerce, the U.S. petroleum industry has been particularly impacted by the imposition of sanctions. Just since World War II, sanctions have been used by the U.S. against Argentina, Venezuela, Libya, Iraq, Iran, China, North Korea, Panama, Haiti, Egypt, South Africa, Angola, Nigeria, Sudan, Algeria, the USSR, Vietnam, Myanmar, Sri Lanka, India, Pakistan, Chile and Cuba. In virtually all of these cases, the participants in the international oil industry have been forced to alter their way of doing business by ceasing oil supply, foregoing investment opportunities, refusing to lift crude oil, stopping cash flow, eliminating travel and taking all possible measures to comply with U.S. law.

The issues surrounding sanctions are not simple ones. While the sanctions are certainly less traumatic than bombs and rockets, they can inflict their own type of pain. And while sanctions may be politically very popular in the U.S. and thus very attractive to their proponents, they have usually not been very effective in achieving their intended results.

On April 28, 1995, two panels of specialists and practitioners in the fields of economics and business, as well as in foreign and defense policy, met at the American Enterprise Institute for Public Policy Research to examine whether economic sanctions designed to pressure states to alter their behavior toward neighboring countries or their own citizens are a useful instrument of U.S. foreign policy.

Texaco, a major international oil company incorporated in the U.S. but doing business in some 150 other countries, has had a great deal of experience living under circumstances in which two sets of (often very different) laws apply. Obviously, for Texaco as a corporation, U.S. law is inviolate. But for employees of Texaco who are citizens of and work in other countries, the situation is not so clear. The American Enterprise Institute forum thus offered an important opportunity to speak out on economic sanctions.

MILEPOST: APRIL 28, 1995

Do Sanctions Work?

American Enterprise Institute for Public Policy Research

———

While the foreign relations landscape may have changed dramatically in the past decade, a discussion of economic sanctions continues to be relevant. Such sanctions include wide-reaching actions such as an embargo on the import or export of all or selected weapons and commodities, the blocking or freezing of assets of a target country, the interruption of international financial transactions and the movement or transportation of goods in or out of said country. In some cases, sanctions have been extended to be made applicable to foreign companies based upon United States stock ownership. As the reach of sanctions has been extended we have, on occasion, strained our relations with our closest allies, particularly in cases where the United States law or regulation is in conflict with that of the allied country and the United States government seeks to enforce its own laws in such country.

Experience has demonstrated that unilateral sanctions are usually ineffective. In cases where the United States has imposed unilateral sanctions, other countries have been all too eager to pick up the resulting economic opportunities. Except where the national security of the United States is threatened, and the President makes a determination to that effect, unilateral sanctions should be avoided. Thus, the United States in contemplating economic sanctions should seek the broadest collaboration of other countries, particularly those countries capable of filling gaps in the economy of the target country resulting from sanctions.

Of course, the potential for sanctions with other countries joining in is in almost direct relationship to the strength of leadership by the United States in the international sphere. The dissolution of the Soviet Union and the return to freedom of the East European countries—resulting in a multi-polar international community in contrast to the earlier bi-polar world—has detracted from focused objectives that emphasized United States leadership generally in international issues. So, the task in mobilizing broad collaboration is difficult indeed, as the recent United States effort to enlarge sanctions against Libya and Iran has demonstrated.

Notwithstanding the problems involved in economic sanctions, the United States will surely apply them in the future. In developing a sanctions program against a target country, planning should include the likelihood of achieving the desired objective, the effect upon the civilian population, the effect on the U.S. economy particularly, and the loss of existing private investment and future opportunity.

> **Economic sanctions clearly have a place in the arsenal of actions available to defend our country and carry out its mission in the world.**

Economic sanctions clearly have a place in the arsenal of actions available to defend our country and carry out its mission in the world. When our national security is directly involved, when American lives are at stake, when our loyal allies are at risk, when our economic strength is threatened, then properly applied economic sanctions must be devised and used.

Specific, enforceable, meaningful sanctions, joined in by all significant powers, have at least a chance of achieving an end. Vague, unenforceable, unilateral sanctions not only do no good, but harm both the United States Government and large segments of the population of the country being sanctioned. They decrease our moral authority, they enrich small, elite segments of the sanctioned country, and they separate us from our allies. Even though the history of sanctions does not provide much confidence in their success, political reality in the U.S. suggests that they will nonetheless be used. Therefore, they should be imposed in as effective a manner as possible.

Designing sanctions with some chance of success requires careful analysis. Corporations will be involved in the implementation of sanctions, and the corporate role must be considered.

While we all have to recognize that foreign policy issues are often not black-and-white and that foreign policy is constantly evolving, the government has a responsibility to enunciate its policy as clearly as possible, so that companies are not forced, in effect, into second-guessing the government, or making

foreign policy on its behalf, which is not the role of a corporation. Companies are not there to create foreign policy. They are
there to do business, in conformity with United States law and
the laws of countries where they have business relations, and
with ethical standards.

It is the province of government, and not that of private companies, to determine which overall policies in various regions
best suit our country's long-term interests.

If the government concludes that our national interests are
best served by a total absence of United States investment from
a particular country, then so be it. But then this needs to be
made clear to everybody up front. The burden should not be on
American corporations to define policy, or to resolve internal
government policy conflicts, or to second-guess what the
national interest is in a given situation. Good corporate citizenship, like good citizenship in general, involves strict conformity
to the law. But good policymaking, in turn, means crafting laws
and policies that are clear and have a reasonable chance of
achieving our goals.

It's not just business that counts on consistency and
predictability in United States foreign policy. This is something
that the world at large rightly expects from our country. I
believe today we still have a way to go in learning how to define
and apply economic sanctions in ways that aren't unnecessarily
confusing or counterproductive for business, or detrimental to
our national credibility as a whole. And I emphasize that U.S.
companies doing business in foreign countries should not be
placed in a position of non-compliance with a law in the host
country in order to comply with United States laws.

With these comments in mind, there are some specific situations to discuss:

Cuba

Since January 1, 1959, the United States has imposed economic
sanctions on Cuba, first because of the nationalization of
United States property in Cuba, and later because of the very
real national security threat posed by the Soviet presence in
Cuba, and by the Cuban adventures abroad. In the early days,
these sanctions were necessary and effective, but they have
done nothing to dislodge Fidel Castro. He remains in power, he
is apparently personally not unpopular in Cuba, and although

his regime, coupled with the sanctions, has impoverished a generation of Cubans, the regime is not ready to fall to the pressure of sanctions.

Now that the Soviet Union no longer poses a threat, it may be time to try a new approach to the rehabilitation of this island nation 90 miles from Florida. Selective relaxation of sanctions, and expansion of trade, tourism, and television, could be an effective formula toward bringing Cuba back into the family of nations. Since the existing sanctions system hasn't worked, and since the military threat no longer exists, a new approach is warranted.

Iraq

Iraq's invasion of Kuwait posed a very real threat to our national security, as well as worldwide security. The United States is greatly dependent on a large, steady supply of crude oil at a competitive price. With some 25 percent of the world's reserves, the Middle East controls the world's supply balance and, therefore, price. Multilateral sanctions on Iraq, followed by military action, were totally appropriate under the circumstances and because of the worldwide threat there was broad collaboration with the United States-led effort. As we have seen, however, sanctions alone rarely bring about a change in government.

Thus, military containment, embargo of weapons of war and mass destruction, and support of Kuwait, Saudi Arabia, and the Emirates by diplomatic and by military means, and the continuing support of our allies represent a course of action which is more likely to defend our interests.

Iran

Again, fourteen years of sanctions have not removed the theocracy governing Iran.* It is important to prevent Iran from having weapons of mass destruction. Toward this end, diplomatic pressure by the United States administration must be placed on Russia to dissuade them from transferring nuclear equipment and technology. Likewise, embargo of war

---

* *And six years after I gave this speech, one could argue that the continuation of the sanctions is undermining the more moderate, elected government in its struggle with the fundamentalist elements.*

materials, strong support from our allies and multinational military containment should be put in place. An oil embargo would probably be ineffective; the oil market is so large, oil is generally fungible, and foreign traders are so adept at circumvention, that even a slight price concession can move large volumes of oil, benefiting the elements we least wish to benefit. A better course would be to concentrate on what is really important: denying Iran arms and nuclear capability.

Thus, the issue of whether or not sanctions are an appropriate instrument of foreign policy, under what conditions they should be used, and how such sanctions should be constructed are all important matters which should continue to receive the benefit of public debate.

Alternative perspectives on energy policy

U.S. policies on economic sanctions, and on other matters that impact energy policy and energy companies, are heavily influenced by a sense that this country is such a major producer that it enjoys significant freedom of action. Not every nation is in that situation, so we can perhaps learn something from how others approach the same issues.

France, for example, finds itself in a radically different situation than the United States with respect to energy supply—and takes a radically different approach. France has little domestic fuel supply; there is limited oil production, and what coal is available is mined at a very high cost. France therefore takes a practical view of various issues in the energy industry. The French have led the world in the percentage of electricity demand that is met through nuclear power; of necessity, they have dealt successfully with the political and engineering problems of nuclear plants, problems that seem much more daunting to the U.S.

It was therefore both interesting and appropriate that in 1993 the French government convened in Paris an energy conference called "Signals for the Future." From literally all over the world, the conference drew economists, civil servants, writers, energy company leaders and technical experts to discuss and study both the history and the future of energy supply. Dr. James Schlesinger, former U.S. secretary of defense and of energy, invited me to the conference to cover these issues from the point of view of an American international oil company. It was a good chance to put on paper a short study of a tumultuous 20 years in the industry, to stress the importance of the free market in allocating resources, and to offer some positive ideas for the future.

MILEPOST: DECEMBER 9, 1993

An Internationalist Perspective on Energy Markets

'Signals for the Future' Energy Conference, Paris

———————

The past 20 years have been a period of unprecedented challenge and crisis for the global oil industry. During this time, the industry has undergone profound change. That's due as much to geopolitical and environmental events as to economic trends.

Throughout this period, there have been numerous misguided attempts by governments to impose inefficient and often politically inspired policies on the oil and gas markets.

In spite of this, the petroleum industry has been able to respond to these major changes with improved strategies, efficiency and technology. And this has allowed it to continue to provide the bulk of the clean, affordable energy that is needed to power the world economy and meet the rising aspirations of people for improved living standards.

As a result, the global oil industry of 1993 is more efficient and effective than ever before. And it's well prepared to face new challenges and uncertainties in the years ahead.

But it's been a rough and rocky road that got us to this point. A road marked by four distinct periods since the end of World War II:

- First, there was 1945–1970, a period characterized by growth.
- Then came the turbulence of 1970–1981, which saw widespread nationalization and price controls, and a radical transformation of the oil industry.
- In reaction, the period 1981–1986 was marked by industry consolidation.
- And finally, the present period, 1986–1993, one of pragmatism and growing recognition of the realities of the world energy situation.

That brings us up to the beginning of 1994. Where is the world oil industry going from here? And what can we do to make sure that it continues to serve the people of the world as efficiently and effectively as possible?

Well, I tend to be an optimist. And one thing I've found out after 40 years in this business is that we definitely can learn from the mistakes of the past, if we're willing to.

And there are several lessons from the events of the past 20 years that I believe will serve us well in the future.

The primary lesson is that the free-market system fulfills consumer needs better than government mandates do. It's been demonstrated pretty convincingly that the free market system best reflects the desires of consumers and the realities of supply and demand.

In contrast, government-imposed mandates, no matter how well-intentioned, are the residue of a discredited command-and-control philosophy, which has failed to work, again and again, in country after country. And too often, these mandates are based on political expediency.

For example, as disruptive as they were at first, the dramatic price increases from the 1973–74 Arab oil embargo resulted in both a permanent improvement in energy efficiency, and an increase in and diversification of crude oil supplies.

In the U.S., the government's reaction to the embargo confirmed the abandonment of a pro-production Federal petroleum policy that had been in place for decades.

But the embargo did not affect oil import volumes in the U.S. to the extent popularly believed. In truth, the shortages there were aggravated by misdirected government intervention.

As a result, the U.S. domestic energy crisis reflected in part the politically inspired failure to allow the market to allocate supplies.

Another lesson we can learn is the need for rigorous testing of proposed solutions to problems, and the need for society to avoid hasty or ill-considered responses.

In determining the best approach to environmental or other problems, solutions ought to be subjected to strict cost-benefit analysis and scientific testing for effectiveness.

For the fact is that all approaches that add costs—whether through higher prices or taxation—will eventually be paid for by the consumer. Such approaches will also sap the economic competitiveness of the industries they affect, cost jobs, and divert society's finite resources from other pressing needs. Therefore, the most cost-effective approaches should be chosen, as well as the most scientifically sound approaches.

As a corollary to that, I'd like to point out that conservation, which has been made ever more practicable by technological advances, is one of the best approaches to resolving environmental and supply issues.

I think that we'll be seeing more and more thoughtful people—in industry and government—embracing the principles of conservation in the future.

I also think we, as an industry, have learned a lot about coping with turmoil and change in the last 20 years. We've learned that, as important as planning and forecasting are, we can never anticipate every event. Sometimes instinct and courage count as much as planning and experience.

Overall, oil industry response to the great shocks of the past two decades has been one of trial and error, and ultimately, that's produced sensible and reasonable adjustments to the new realities of the global energy market.

> **Sometimes instinct and courage count as much as planning and experience.**

At first, if you remember, companies diversified into a wide range of energy and other enterprises. They included coal and copper mines, shale oil and tar sands, and some totally unrelated activities. And all of them were failures.

Companies also pursued over-aggressive exploration in the expectation of $100-a-barrel oil. Well, as we're all too aware, the $100 price never materialized.

It's pretty evident now that a much better approach for the industry would have been to modernize our refineries, so we could use the lowest-cost feedstock, while also pursuing cost-effective exploration around the world.

For a time, exploratory activity, based on unrealistic price expectations, also produced an uneconomic allocation of capital by the companies, particularly in the U.S.

More conservative forecasts would have suggested that the companies develop only that oil that could be produced competitively.

Today, in this age of realism, oil companies are following the strategies of cost control, as well as continued research in all areas of the business. At the same time, the international oil industry is re-integrating, between upstream and downstream companies.

As we turn to the future, it's growing increasingly important that the people of the world, and their leaders, recognize that the oil industry has powered the unprecedented progress of the 20th Century. And, even more important, that our industry remains a valuable asset for the economies of the world.

Because the fact is, oil will be the predominant source of energy for the foreseeable future. Despite all the talk about new sources, the hard fact is that there simply are no feasible alternatives on the horizon.

Therefore, the proven ability of the oil companies to do the job, and the formidable technology at hand and under development, make the global oil industry essential to meeting the world's future economic, energy and environmental needs.

It's important that we learn from what's happened over the last 20 years, and learn from the mistakes of the past. Certainly, there is plenty of blame to be shared for those mistakes. In industry as well as in government.

So rather than dwell on them, it would be wise for all interested parties—the oil companies as well as governments, opinion leaders and various interests—to respect each other's point of view. And to work together for the common good.

The greatest lesson of all is that the challenges are major. It's important that all of us in positions of public responsibility consult and cooperate if the global oil industry is to serve the best interests of the people of the world. They're relying on us for the energy they need for a better life.

■

An absolute necessity

In this chapter we have reviewed the origins of the Gulf War and its impact on at least one company; the interrelationships between the oil industry and the military; the use of sanctions as a tool of national will; and the lessons offered by the events of the past 30 years in the area of petroleum supply.

These are four seemingly separate concerns, but a strong common thread runs through them. For it is obvious that a secure supply of affordable energy is an absolute necessity for human society—and has been, since man discovered fire.

As I think over what we have learned over the past 30 years (and over the past 150 years, for that matter), several conclusions are apparent:

- Oil is and was important to our economy and to our international relations—and thus must play a part in national strategic thinking for the foreseeable future.
- The free market is superior to all other systems in its ability to allocate supplies and to direct the development of new sources of energy.
- Economic warfare, particularly of the unilateral variety, is usually unsuccessful.
- Producing states and consuming states alike have an interest in stable, long-term relationships for which to date the only substitute has been the aircraft carrier task force.

Thus our energy security rests on innovative technology at home, diversity of supply abroad, continuous and effective diplomacy, and a strong military ready and available wherever needed.

7

Environmental and Regulatory Challenges

O ne of the defining problems in the latter half of the 20th Century was the environment; we can safely assume it will only be more important in the 21st Century. Air pollution, water contamination and land degradation have become deeply felt concerns for all who care about the quality, and indeed the sustainability, of human life.

These issues have in turn become the basis for strong political forces that have had enormous impact on the world's great industrial corporations. This is a challenge that industry must address by doing what industry is best at—innovative problem-solving, and technological leadership.

Industrial advances are almost automatically blamed for pollution and other environmental problems. Yet advanced technology is more often the solution than the problem. Technology to ameliorate environmental damage has come a long way, and it will represent a fertile area for research (and for sound business investment) for many years to come.

For example, technology is making possible ever more efficient uses of energy. And conservation—though not always popular—remains one of the best methods of pollution control. It is particularly important in addressing concerns about global warming, which is attributed to carbon dioxide created by the burning of fossil fuels.

Today's homes—with insulation, double-glazed windows, timer-operated thermostats, fuel-efficient furnaces, new materials and other technological advances—use less energy per cubic foot of space than their predecessors, and they are more comfortable as well. Automobiles today are much safer than cars of only two decades ago, yet they are more fuel-efficient and pollute far less. In fact, passenger-car miles driven in the United States more than doubled between 1976 and 1996, yet the air became significantly cleaner. For the next generation, hybrid cars that combine an internal combustion engine with an electric motor promise further improvements in fuel efficiency and air quality, as do fuel-cell powered vehicles.

Simply because of the greater scale of their economic activity, the industrialized nations currently create more pollution than do the emerging economies. But the environmental technologies the U.S. and other advanced countries are developing offer a realistic hope that the poorer nations of the world can grow their economies without undue harm to the global ecology.

Raw materials, energy, forests, land and water cannot continue to be wasted, particularly in the United States, where continued profligate use of seemingly endless supplies of these treasures must be balanced against our desire for an attractive quality of life for our descendants.

Texaco adopted a slogan that might have seemed a strange one for an oil company—but one that effectively communicated the concept of a wiser use of resources: "Conservation: let's put our energy into saving it."

Some activists, of course, portray the oil industry as a kind of dinosaur, out of place in a rapidly changing world. Yet the truth is that the technological prowess and environmental impact of the oil industry are changing rapidly, too. The industry stands to prosper, not wither away, as human society makes wiser use of the power and promise of its energy resources.

The oil industry can successfully advance, however, only in concert with the industries that make use of its products—especially the auto industry. From the invention of the automobile powered by the internal combustion engine in the latter part of the 19th Century, the oil industry and the auto industry have had a symbiotic relationship. Obviously the auto industry could not survive without the oil industry; today's automobiles do not work without petroleum. It is only slightly less obvious that the oil industry is dependent upon the automobile; automotive use represents the largest single market for the lighter fractions of crude oil.

So where these two industries go, they go together. For example, drivability concerns in the 1930s led the auto industry to increase engine compression ratios; therefore the oil industry changed its fuels to offer higher octane levels. But then in the 1970s the auto industry began employing catalytic converters to oxidize unburned hydrocarbons in a car's exhaust stream and thus reduce its pollution. So the oil industry phased down and finally eliminated the use of tetraethyl lead—a component that boosted octane, but poisoned the catalytic converters.

Still, for years the "autos" and the "oils" (as the two industries call each other) never formally sat down together to design the best possible combination of automobile and fuel which, taken together, would minimize pollution while maximizing consumer satisfaction relative to performance, initial cost, maintenance cost, fuel cost and automobile longevity.

Nor did governmental policies do anything to encourage such collaboration. The Federal Clean Air Act of 1970 was landmark legislation that did a great deal to enhance environmental quality, especially in the early years when the easiest and cheapest fixes were adopted. But it also set a pattern for a command-and-control approach to environmental regulation in which government has increasingly tended to lay down highly detailed specifications for products and processes, without first undertaking the kind of cost/benefit analysis that would identify the most cost-effective method of achieving a given level of environmental improvement.

Cost/benefit analysis is never easy. But in its absence, the governmental decision-making process tends to evolve into a political contest among interest groups, each seeking to extract a benefit or avoid a cost for itself, without reference to the most cost-effective solution for the environment and the society as a whole.

Political logrolling in the name of the environment, for example, has led to massive subsidies for the use of ethanol in automotive fuel. Ethanol is an alcohol made from corn. It is the active ingredient in whiskey, where its efficacy is beyond question. Its use in motor fuel, however, is highly debatable. Ethanol production consumes more energy than is contained in the resultant product. Ethanol-containing fuels cannot be shipped by pipeline. Ethanol produces toxic combustion products. Subsidizing it does no real good for the environment, but it is good for the farm vote. In the absence of cost/benefit analysis, that's how environmental policy tends to be made.

Another good example is the debate over maintenance requirements to ensure that automobiles continue meeting the environmental standards they were designed for. It is well documented that the oldest, most poorly maintained 10 percent of the automotive fleet produces 50 percent of the automotive pollutants. Mandatory inspection and maintenance would be one of the most cost-effective ways of reducing atmospheric pollution. Why isn't it the law? Because of political concerns that this would be a regulatory cost that voters would see—as opposed to the costs they don't see, such as the impact of tougher regulations on the cost of gasoline and of new cars.

With the political decision-making process caught in this dysfunctional pattern, Texaco decided in the spring of 1989 that it was time to show some leadership. In an address to the Economic Club of Detroit, which is one of the country's most important platforms and is located in the home of the automobile, we suggested a joint study by the oil and automotive industries.

Our proposal was unconventional, but it produced results. In the fall of 1989 the two industries established the Auto/Oil Air Quality Improvement Research Program. Its objective was to provide data to help legislators and regulators achieve the nation's clean-air goals through research that would include:

- Extensive vehicle emission measurements.
- Air-quality modeling studies to predict the effects of the emissions on ozone formation.
- And economic analysis of various fuel/vehicle systems.

With expenditures by the companies of over $40 million between 1989 and 1992, the program was the largest and most comprehensive project of this nature ever conducted. It produced findings that have been equally valuable to industry and to all levels of government— without which there would simply have been no scientific basis for the expensive, wide-scale pollution control programs that elected officials were being asked to enact. But this collaboration did not entirely lay to rest the tug-of-war between the "autos" and the "oils." Oil companies continued to advocate vehicle modifications that would reduce pollution while using existing fuels, and the auto manufacturers continued to press for expensive new fuels in place of those modifications.

MILEPOST: MAY 1, 1989

Industry Collaboration in Environmental Improvement

Address to The Economic Club of Detroit, Michigan

For most of our lifetimes, the auto companies that make their home here have sat side-by-side with the oil companies on the top of the industrial world. We grew up together in the early days of this century—and we fueled each others' explosive growth.

We cooperated as our markets grew and our technology became more sophisticated—working together to establish technical standards that have helped consumers get the most out of both of our products, and maintaining an ongoing dialogue. The forging of these strong bonds was only natural—after all, we need each other.

To give you an idea of how much we depend on each other, let me note that in 1988 gasoline sales represented 53 percent of Texaco's total U.S. product revenue—not to mention the 300 million quarts of motor oil we sold. And of course, only an infinitesimal percentage of Detroit's cars use anything but gasoline, and all use some form of lubricants.

Working together, we have made the automobile the defining symbol of 20th Century America.

Unfortunately, since the 1970s, our world seems to be turning more rapidly—and comfortable and successful working relationships have come under some strain. Thickening smog over many of our cities has raised the question of how the responsibility and the burden of ensuring a future of clean, breathable air will be borne.

The answer I want to offer today is: "By all of us—together." All of us in industry need to step up and bear our share of the burden of ensuring a clean environment. No one can be more aware of the extent of that responsibility than the oil industry, following the regrettable incident involving a tanker at Valdez.

Unfortunately, in the area of clean air, our inability to settle the issue of the optimum environmental control strategy among ourselves has encouraged others to settle it for us—at a greater than necessary cost to future prosperity and national security. And unless we literally and promptly get our act together, the world as we know it may be about to turn over on us.

I raise this alarm in reaction to a rapidly developing piece of conventional wisdom: that the gasoline engine has become a dinosaur that will not survive the need for stricter environmental standards.

This view is based on two assumptions, increasingly forwarded by environmental interests:

The first assumption is that nearly all the improvement possible in controlling emissions has been wrung out of the gasoline engine. A recent article in *The New York Times* quoted federal environmental officials to the effect that 96 percent of all hydrocarbon emissions has been removed—and that any further gains would be incremental. Since several high-population-density areas remain far out of compliance with Clean Air Act standards, this view states, America will have to look to alternative fuels for improvement. Unfortunately, this view overlooks the fact that a high percentage of cars currently on the road today fall far short of removing 96 percent of hydrocarbon emissions.

The second assumption is that a number of alternative fuels could provide the necessary improvement in ozone levels at a reasonable cost to society. This assumption is also incorrect.

The degree to which this new conventional wisdom is gaining acceptance is brought home even more dramatically by the recent air quality plan adopted by California's South Coast Air Quality Management District.

The Southern California plan is an appropriately wide-ranging attack on air quality problems that have left the region far out of compliance with Clean Air Act mandates. It involves controls on everything from backyard barbecues to drive-throughs at McDonald's. Air problems in L.A., as we all know, are compounded by the city's location in a vast bowl, under a temperature inversion, which has the effect of trapping pollutants.

But the feature of the plan that should really raise eyebrows is the provision which would require that all cars in the Los

Angeles basin be converted to electric power or other "clean" fuels by the year 2007.

There's no question that dramatic action must be taken in Southern California and elsewhere in the nation to meet Clean Air Act requirements—given the potential threat to the continued health and productivity of the people of Southern California and other densely populated regions.

But I do believe that the California plan, which has fanned the flames of the raging debate on how to achieve air quality, offers our industries a joint opportunity to propose alternative approaches—approaches that will achieve equal or better results than those projected for these alternative fuels, at much less cost to society. It is imperative that we seize this opportunity, because it is so important to the future health and welfare of our two industries and our country.

Today, I would like to discuss how the oil and auto industries can take advantage of that opportunity—and to call on the leaders of our industries to work together in formulating just such an alternative approach.

> **The California plan offers our industries a joint opportunity to propose alternative approaches.**

Strong auto and oil industries are vital to America's economic strength, as well as its national security. We must not forget the lessons of the past 15 years.

First, however, I believe we need to examine the new conventional wisdom about the benefits of eliminating the gasoline engine in favor of alternative fuels—and analyze the true impact of that approach on the nation.

Let's address the assumption that alternative fuels can provide the improvements in emissions sought under the Clean Air Act.

Several alternative fuels have been considered—and all present substantial problems, both of a technical and practical nature.

I don't need to tell anyone in Detroit about the enormous technical problems that stand between the electric engine and the consumer market.

But I would point out that electric vehicles would also add to the demands on an electric generating system already so strained that we may have to undergo selective brownouts to get through this summer. Moreover, expanding the capacity of that system would involve either the burning of more coal, with its own emission problems, or turning to nuclear power, which the U.S. has proven unwilling to do.

So until now, the favorite of the alternative fuels proponents has been methanol.

But the fact is, no solid data exist demonstrating emissions improvement in methanol engines. Certainly none were cited by the California South Coast air quality district. And as many of you are no doubt aware, methanol presents its own unique set of environmental, safety, and national security problems:

  - First, methanol emissions produce three to five times as much formaldehyde as gasoline. Formaldehyde is a strongly reactive emission in terms of ozone formation—meaning that it is a strong contributor to that process wherever it is present. Equally troubling, formaldehyde has been categorized as a probable carcinogen by the EPA.
  - Second, because methanol is so corrosive, methanol engines cannot be guaranteed for even 50,000 miles with today's technology. It's possible that cars would lose emissions control capability much more quickly with methanol—leading to sharply increased emissions as cars age.

The investment cost alone of meeting the methanol needs of just this minuscule percentage of the California market—a far smaller percentage than the population of the Los Angeles basin, and only five-tenths of a percent of the entire U.S. market— would be up to $1.5 billion.

The obvious question is where this dimension of new investment in methanol, electric engines, or other alternative fuels is going to come from—especially given the many unanswered questions about their feasibility and environmental benefits. Especially when the California plan contemplates that methanol is to be replaced by all-electric cars in 20 years. How many people will be willing to invest billions of dollars in a business to be shut down in 20 years?*

After all, very recent history reminds us that exactly such kinds of major investments have been made in alternative energy technologies. Do the words "shale" and "solar" ring a bell—not to mention nuclear power?

---

* *Eleven years later, methanol is no longer seen as a fuel for internal combustion engines.*

Taxpayers, ratepayers and shareholders are still paying for mega-billion dollar investments made—and later abandoned—when these solutions proved economically, technologically, or politically unworkable.

The motorists of America, many of whom depend on cars to commute to work, would pay a heavy price for any complications or delays that may stem from installing a methanol distribution system to fuel methanol cars rolling off the assembly lines.

It seems to me that part of the problem surrounding these alternative technologies was that government policymakers and private industry alike rushed in without sufficient time for study and consultation to ensure that these solutions were feasible, affordable, and truly necessary over the long term.

The question now is, will we see another huge government program mandating investment in methanol or electric cars before all the facts are in? And if we do, who will be stuck with the bill if these alternatives go bust?

While, on the one hand, we are seeing a rush to judgment on alternative technologies, there seems to be a curious reluctance to re-examine the second threshold assumption I raised a few minutes ago—that all the potential emission improvements have already been squeezed out of gasoline engines.

It's curious because this assumption rests on flawed environmental standards and testing. Actually, we need more accurate emission measurements for automobiles in actual highway and city use—as opposed to running at rest.

The fact is, evidence exists that emissions of unburned hydrocarbons in actual highway use may be considerably higher than predicted by current test methods.

And if this is true, it seems to me that such improvements to current designs are much more feasible, and probably easier to achieve, than a totally redesigned engine and distribution system.

There is also a second factor undermining the assumption that we have achieved all the emission improvements possible for gasoline engines. The fact is, political sensitivities have halted proposals to introduce and implement regulations requiring careful maintenance of emissions systems by car owners.

It seems to me that we should consider asking motorists to bear the reasonable costs of achieving improved emissions through improved maintenance—before we impose on them and the rest of society the unknowable costs of an entirely new generation of automotive and fuel technologies.

The bottom line of all of this is relatively simple and straight-forward: before we go down the garden path of massive invest-ment in unproved technologies—before we turn the world over on ourselves—I believe that we need to examine more fully the issue of whether the emissions improvement needed to assure healthy air can be achieved by a redesigned clean emissions system based on the existing gasoline engine.

I don't make this statement as an excuse for stalling. This problem of meeting clean air standards, and our responsibility to help solve the problem, are too big, too real, and too immediate for us to respond with anything but a sincere sense of urgency.

Rather, I want to make a call for action: joint action involving executives at the very top of the oil and automotive industries.

Specifically, I want to propose today a joint effort between the oil and automotive industries to address and solve the prob-lem of a sufficiently cleaner emission system to meet EPA stan-dards—within the timeframe and limits mandated by the California plan—and in a way that divides the responsibility appropriately between our two industries.

On that latter point, those of you representing the automo-tive industry may have noticed that I used the term "cleaner emissions system"—as opposed to "cleaner engine." Implicit in that term is the recognition that solving the problem of clean, breathable air for tomorrow involves not only investment by Detroit in more efficient engines, but also investment by the oil industry in less volatile fuels and better controls in storage and distribution systems.

To meet this objective, I want to propose the following steps:

- First, an early series of meetings of top officers from the oil and auto industries to map out a program and coordinate resources aimed at presenting a joint proposal for a more cost-effective alternative strategy to the California Air Resources Board within the very near future.
- Second, the commitment of staff and resources from our companies to carry out a comprehensive series of studies and new technical research and, ultimately, to propose new automotive and gasoline technologies which, working together, will allow the gasoline engines and automotive fuels of tomorrow to attain or exceed clean air standards.

At Texaco, we stand ready to commit the resources and time needed not only to respond to the call for alternative approaches in California, but to the search for a comprehensive long-term solution. Today, I urge my counterparts in the auto and oil industries to join me in making this commitment.

I would remind my friends in the auto industry that our industries have worked cooperatively—and achieved mightily—for most of our histories.

Today we cannot afford to sit on the sidelines and boo at alternative approaches to the challenge of providing a clean environment, or seek to pass the buck. We must meet this challenge ourselves—rising above past differences and old approaches—to challenge the conventional wisdom, and to provide positive direction in a cooperative effort with authorities we have often viewed as adversaries.

But I am convinced that if we can renew and expand the dialogue we have enjoyed in the past, we can meet the challenge facing us—and build on the legacy of greatness that is ours as the leaders of two of America's most vital industries.

Because of our cooperation throughout this century, our products have moved the world—literally. Today, by working together, I believe we can move the world to an even brighter and cleaner future—ensuring prosperity, energy security, and a higher quality of life for generations to come.

Taking the message directly to California

California is the birthplace of environmental initiatives that then migrate across our country and around the world—much as the prevailing winds over the United States blow from west to east.

There are many reasons it plays this role. California is a huge and captivatingly beautiful state, with mountain ranges, quiet deserts and coastal landscapes that are among the world's most pristine. Yet it is also the most populous state in the Union, and it continues to grow rapidly.

The demands of 33 million consumers inevitably are framed against the backdrop of the state's physical beauty. That long and splendid coastline, for example, also represents the border of a major marine shipping lane traversed by tankers providing crude oil and refined products to a state that leads the nation in energy consumption.

Even the sunny, balmy climate in Los Angeles comes with a price. The region has a unique air pollution problem, because of a geography that traps emitted materials in an atmospheric inversion layer, in which all that sunlight sets off a reaction creating smog. This is not entirely a new phenomenon; the native people referred to the region as the Valley of the Smokes. But with its growing population and its love affair with the car, Southern California today has a very real air problem that has to be addressed.

Much of Southern California is also a desert, and fresh water supplies must come by diversion from the Colorado River in the east and by aqueducts from the north. Clean, fresh water may not seem like an environmental "problem" to those who live where it is plentiful—but when you have to build dams and aqueducts to supply it, it can be.

In Northern California are the world's last remaining stands of Sequoias, magnificent trees that were living at the time of Christ. The competing needs of commercial lumbering interests, and of those dedicated to preserving these unique wonders of nature, meet there head-on.

In addition to being a large consumer of energy, California is a major producing state. Oil production at Signal Hill and at Kern River goes back over a century. But newer discoveries in the Santa Barbara Channel have for 30 years sparked an on-going war between the producers, and those who want the benefits of petroleum but do not want it produced in their home town.

Seen from the nearby hills, the illuminated oil platforms off the shore of Santa Barbara remind some Californians of the Great White Fleet, proud examples of our country's industrial might. But in the minds of others, they are constant reminders of an oil industry they perceive as a villain.

The fact is that perception quickly becomes reality—particularly in dealing with environmental issues, and not just in California. I first learned this lesson in the 1950s, working in Puerto Rico. Kerosene was still a big seller on the island in those days, used for cooking and for lighting in many homes where electricity was not yet available. Purity was a big selling point, and adjectives that translated as "water white" and "crystallite" were often used when touting the product.

All of our kerosene in San Juan was stored in a single, 42,000-barrel tank. One day our product, seemingly all at once, acquired a yellowish tinge. Kerosene with such a color wouldn't sell because the customers would believe it had been adulterated with some cheaper material, such as diesel oil, and would surely smoke up their houses. Samples were sent to our Texas lab, and it tested pure. But the fact remained, it didn't *look* pure. What to do?

The laboratory suggested trying to bleach the entire batch, and sent along several pounds of potassium permanganate—which, when dissolved in benzene, makes a powerful dark blue oxidizing agent.

The foreman of the tank farm and I took our drum of treated benzene and jury-rigged a hose from the drum to the gauge hatch on the tank and then started to circulate the material, sampling as we went along. Slowly, slowly, the yellow began to fade. But just when success seemed in hand, our sample suddenly turned light blue! We had slightly overdone our oxidizing and were now faced with 42,000 barrels of a lovely blue kerosene.

I was horrified by what I had done. But our sales people rescued me. They dubbed the product *"kerosina azul,"* and they predicted that customers would far prefer it to our competitors' clear white product. They were right; sales were never better. Somehow blue was associated in the public's mind with purity; yellow was not. There was no actual difference in the purity of the product. But that was how the public saw things, and that was that.

I cannot say that we ever made any more blue kerosene, but I never forgot that the public's perception is a reality that is ignored only at your peril.

The public perception of industry's environmental record was foremost in my mind when, in 1990, I was invited to address the Commonwealth Club of California.

Hard Thinking on the Best Approach to Environmental Progress

Address to the Commonwealth Club of California, San Francisco

―――――――――

I always enjoy visiting your city and the Bay area. There's a great vitality here. It comes from being in the vanguard of social and intellectual trends. Yet there's also a sense of history, an appreciation of the past, that gives this area its special character.

What I want to talk to you about are two imperatives—one as old as history, the other compelling as the future. They are the age-old aspiration of people everywhere for a better life for themselves and their children, and the very real concerns we all have for the future of the earth's environment.

Sam Goldwyn once advised, "Never make forecasts—especially about the future!" I won't be making any predictions today. But I do have a few ideas and a few insights that might be useful, as we try to come to grips with these imperatives.

I've just come back from the Far East. And as we were flying over the Pacific, I started to think about my first trip out there, during the Korean War, as a brand-new ensign out of the Naval Academy.

I remember so clearly when I reported to my ship, the *U.S.S. Badoeng Strait*. The thing that struck me about life aboard ship was the sense of community. How the ship was a self-contained world, steaming through hostile waters. And all of us in the crew were in it together, each man depending on his shipmates.

Living space was pretty tight. So we had to be especially considerate of each other. If somebody was noisy, or didn't keep his quarters clean, there was no place you could go to get away from him.

It occurred to me that this is really the situation all of us find ourselves in, in our world today. Like the crew of the *U.S.S. Badoeng Strait*, we also live aboard an increasingly cramped ship, the planet Earth, floating in a sea of space. Our resources, including air and water, are limited.

More and more, what people do in one part of the world affects the rest of us. Incidents such as Chernobyl, or actions such as cutting down the Brazilian rain forest, have an impact everywhere.

I think this realization has taken hold throughout the world in the past few years. That's led to a fundamental change in attitudes toward our resources and the environment. Environmental quality is no longer the sole province of activists. By now, it's become a central issue—perhaps *the* central issue—of the '90s. Around the world, people are deeply concerned about the environment—and rightly so.

As an individual, I welcome this. I spend a lot of time outdoors. And I want to see the natural beauty of this earth preserved, so that my children and theirs will also be able to enjoy it.

But as the head of one of the world's major energy companies, I'm also aware of the potential conflict between environmental needs and people's aspirations for a better life.

Three hundred years ago, the British philosopher, Thomas Hobbes, described life for most of mankind as "solitary, poor, nasty, brutish and short." And it really wasn't until this century that this changed for most Americans.

Today, we tend to take our modern conveniences and standard of living for granted. And now, people all over the world—in Latin America, in Eastern Europe, in rural Asia—are increasingly demanding those things that make life better: cars, electric lights, refrigerators, air conditioning, central heating.

And there's the rub. Because all of that requires energy. Lots of energy. And the environmental risks that go along with supplying it.

I've spent my entire business career in the oil industry. I take a lot of pride in the fact that affordable and accessible energy has fueled the economic progress of the past century.

But, like a lot of oil people, I realize that in the years to come, while we're going to provide the fuel for economic growth, we'll have to do it without polluting the environment of our shared planet.

Some are saying it can't be done. That we cannot reconcile the demand for affordable, available energy, which provides high living standards, with the need for a clean environment.

I don't agree. I don't think we're going to have to choose between freezing in cold and darkness, or suffocating in noxious pollution. I don't believe it's a zero-sum game. I think we've shown, again and again, that mankind is a creator of wealth, not just a consumer of it. And that if we marshal our scientific and intellectual abilities, we'll be able to have both the energy and the environment we want. Because my concept of wealth includes a clean environment.

But it won't be easy. It's going to require that we face the real facts about energy and the environment, and not be distracted by those with peripheral agendas. We must shed the illusions that have clouded the issue, and weigh the costs and practical benefits of various courses of action, and set priorities. We've all got to start pulling on the same end of the rope—with business, government, and concerned, thoughtful citizens working together in the public interest.

Let's look at some of the facts—coolly and realistically—like Joe Montana fading back and assessing his options.

One fact is supply and demand. Demand for energy is growing, worldwide. And that trend will continue. Since the early 1980s, energy demand in the U.S. alone has grown by almost 2 percent a year.

Demand may rise even faster in the future. Events in western and eastern Europe will spur economic growth. And we estimate that the Pacific Rim, the most rapidly growing area of the world economically, could require an added three million barrels of oil per day by 1995, and as much as two million more by the year 2000.

> **We've all got to start pulling on the same end of the rope— with business, government, and concerned, thoughtful citizens working together in the public interest.**

At the same time, however, it's getting harder and harder to find and develop major sources of crude oil. Here in the U.S., domestic crude oil production has been dropping by about 4 percent a year—6 percent in 1989.

When we do find a major source of crude, such as the one Texaco and other companies found down at Point Arguello, off Santa Barbara, local opposition can prevent its production.

Since we can no longer find and produce all the oil and gas we need in the United States, imports of foreign crude and petroleum products are now filling close to 50 percent of U.S. demand. As a result, the cost of imported oil equates to roughly 44 percent of last year's U.S. trade deficit.

Even if we produced all the oil we consume, we might not be able to refine it. U.S. refineries are running at near capacity now. And they don't cover U.S. demand. Investment in new or expanded refineries is discouraged by uncertainty over disposal restrictions. Those same regulations make it more expensive to refine our products here than abroad. Without new refining capacity, the U.S. is in danger of exporting its refining industry, along with its jobs. There are also implications for national security and our balance of trade.

Those are the facts this nation must face, but hasn't. Instead, we've too often clung to illusions. Illusions that, somehow, there's some miracle fuel lying just beyond the blue horizon. Or that we can find a quick fix to energy and environmental problems, at little cost or inconvenience to us. In other words, a free lunch. Well, I'm afraid it just doesn't work that way.

A year or so ago, there was a new attempt to do something about the very real problem of auto and other emissions in the Los Angeles Basin. The Southern California Air Quality Board proposed an aggressive two-year program.

Early versions of the plan assumed the elimination of motor gasoline. And methanol was decreed as the designated fuel of choice—all before the facts were fully checked out.

Since then, people have been taking a closer look at this idea, and having second thoughts. They've learned, for example, that methanol emissions produce three to five times as much formaldehyde as gasoline. And formaldehyde is a carcinogen and a major contributor to ozone formation.

They've seen that methanol is corrosive, extremely toxic and volatile. That much of it would have to be produced overseas from foreign natural gas. And that converting to it on a mass scale would be monumentally expensive. The cost of new vehicles, new plants and new distribution systems would be immense.

The point is, methanol and its derivatives may well have a place in the future mix of fuels offered to customers. But a lot more research and evaluation are needed before it is determined how big a role they should play.*

We need to take an equally close look at proposals to switch to alternative vehicles, such as electric cars. At first blush, they sound great. Batteries would run these vehicles, and

---

* *One methanol derivative, MTBE, is now being phased out of the gasoline pool for environmental reasons.*

there'd be no tailpipe emissions. But again: the hard facts. Electric cars would be terribly expensive. They'd only go some 75 miles between charges. Recharging would take hours. And the additional electric power to do it would still have to be generated somewhere. We'd just be shifting pollution from the tailpipe to the new power plants.*

Likewise, it is far from certain that alternative energy sources will significantly cut pollution from electric power generation, either. Oil, gas and coal now provide 70 percent of all the energy used to generate electricity in the United States. The realistic outlook is that they will continue to dominate in the foreseeable future. So further cleaning of existing fuels is where the greatest opportunities for pollution control lie.

Nuclear power was once thought to be the fuel of the future. But its opponents are proving fairly successful at shutting down generating plants wherever they can.

The more exotic energy sources—geothermal, solar and wind—provide only 1 or 2 percent of total U.S. energy needs. And they're not likely to account for much for quite some time.

Ironically, even the best-intentioned scheme to produce power is not without environmental risks. For example, there's a big fight going on right now in Hawaii, over a plan to tap into the steam below the Kilauea volcano. It sounds like a great idea: generating 500 megawatts of electricity from natural sources, and freeing Hawaii of its dependence on imported oil. But building the plant would destroy America's last big tropical rain forest. And that would hardly be a plus for the environment.

Not all is darkness and gloom. There has been a lot of progress, and more improvements will come. From my standpoint at Texaco, I can tell you personally that a great deal is going on, right now, to make the production, transportation, refining and use of oil and gas much safer—both environmentally and in terms of human health.

You may remember that in 1969, there was a major oil spill from a well blowout in the Santa Barbara Channel. It shocked the world. And believe me, it shocked the oil industry. So we did

---

*   *This is in contrast to technology now being developed to produce cars that can create their own electricity—through fuel cells, for exemple, or in "hybrid" cars that combine internal combustion and electric engines.*

something about it. Procedures were tightened, preventive measures were beefed up, planning for emergencies was improved.

The results: Since 1970, five billion barrels of oil have been produced from U.S. waters. In that time, there hasn't been one single significant spill resulting from a blowout or offshore producing incident. During this same period, some 37,000 wells have been drilled safely in federal and state waters.

Recent incidents in petroleum transportation have pointed up the need for improvements in that area. The tanker spills at Valdez and, more recently, Huntington Beach, have reverberated throughout the industry. But, as in 1969 with the Santa Barbara drilling incident, we're doing something about it.

We've been working to set up the Petroleum Industry Response Organization, or PIRO. Although some industry groups and cooperatives are already in place with equipment and manpower to respond to moderate spills, more equipment and technology are needed. PIRO will reinforce our capability by assembling and maintaining equipment and personnel at centers around the U.S., to respond to large spills.

Perhaps more important, long term, PIRO will conduct research on cleanup and containment technology. Present methods for dealing with spills are simply not good enough. Overall, the petroleum industry plans to spend more than $400 million over the next five years on PIRO.

Another example of industry's response is that the oil company segment of the U.S. tanker industry, through the American Petroleum Institute, is supporting several initiatives intended to improve marine safety. These include:

- The expansion of, and mandatory participation in, so-called advisory vessel traffic systems, whereby movements of all vessels within defined hazardous areas are monitored by the U.S. Coast Guard.
- The establishment of higher qualifications and improved administrative standards for state harbor pilots.
- A requirement for tugboat assistance or special maneuvering equipment for tankers in areas defined as hazardous.
- An expanded program of drug and alcohol testing and treatment.
- A U.S. Coast Guard review of manning standards aboard tankers.
- And the already ongoing study by the National Academy of Science to review tanker design and recommend changes in

design as a way to reduce oil spills. This study is addressing the important question of a need for double bottoms or double hulls.

But despite Valdez and other unfortunate events, the real story for the oil industry is that there are some 750 million barrels of oil at sea on any given day, supplying much of the fuel needed by motorists and to run the world's industries. Gases and products add more. Incidents—as terrible as they are—are extremely rare. And the petroleum industry is working hard to reduce these occurrences still further, and minimize their impact.

We take our responsibilities to the environment very seriously. Our written corporate principles commit us to be a good steward of the environment. In the last 20 years—since the first "Earth Day"—we've spent hundreds of millions of dollars on environmental equipment and activities. We've created a new environmental, health and safety division, charged with developing the most effective policies and programs for those areas. We've also set up a board-level public responsibility committee that reviews matters affecting the environment, health and safety.

> **We can't hold back the demand for increased energy—and the risk it entails. But we can manage the risks, and minimize them.**

These efforts, by us and other oil companies, have produced results. One small example is at our Habitat production platform, off the California Coast. There, the surrounding ocean is so clean that commercial fishermen harvest mussels off the platform legs and sell them to gourmet restaurants from here to Los Angeles.

There are bigger examples, too. In the U.S., over the past 10 years, ambient airborne lead levels are down 88 percent. Ozone, the leading component of smog, is down 16 percent. Carbon monoxide, 32 percent. Nitrogen oxides, 12 percent. Dust, soot and particulates, 21 percent. And sulfur dioxide is down 35 percent. All this has been accomplished despite an unexpected and unprecedented growth in motor vehicle traffic.

Today's new cars are designed to eliminate almost 97 percent of the volatile polluting elements in the exhaust. New models now in development will trap, contain and get rid of a major portion of the remaining 3 percent. So despite all the bad news we often read about, environmental progress is being made.

But obviously, still more needs to be done. Last spring, I spoke to the Economic Club of Detroit, and proposed that the major players in the oil industry and the automobile industry get together. We could pool our efforts to find cost-effective methods of cutting vehicle emissions by reformulating our fuels and redesigning our cars.

Well, the response was great, and we've got a joint industry task force up and running. And it's making solid progress.

In addition, Texaco is contributing $500,000 to the California Institute of Technology to co-sponsor its new center for air quality analysis. This will be a forum to exchange scientific information on air quality issues, and a valuable resource for joint research on solutions.

In sum, we can't hold back the demand for increased energy—and the risk it entails. But we can manage the risks, and minimize them.

In closing, I want to give you some ideas I have to help society meet the challenges of providing energy while protecting the environment.

First, I think we ought to take immediate action on those things that can be done relatively cheaply and easily.

One is phasing out those cars that are causing most of the automotive air pollution. A study by the University of Denver showed that more than 50 percent of the carbon monoxide problems in that city stemmed from less than 10 percent of the cars—the older and poorly maintained ones. Light trucks, especially those built before 1980, add to this pollution.

Perhaps we should consider incentives for owners to retire their old cars, and tougher inspection and maintenance standards for those still on the road. That appears to present a cost-effective, near-term solution to a high proportion of automotive emissions.

Another common-sense approach would be to design and require pre-heaters on automobile catalytic converters. Studies show that as much as half of all tailpipe pollutants from new cars are emitted before the catalytic converter warms up.*

---

*   *I was so committed to this approach that I personally invented and patented a device for pre-heating converters. This particular device has not gone into production, but newer converters use other technology to bring them to operating temperature more quickly.*

Finally, we've also got to balance legitimate local interests with the equally legitimate interests of society as a whole. For example, in exploring for and producing oil and gas, we have to go where those resources are. Sometimes, that means areas that local people feel are environmentally sensitive. Their feelings are understandable. But let's face it: *All* areas are environmentally sensitive, especially to the people who live there. Yet we all use automobiles, mass transit and electricity. And they all require fuel. So what some folks really seem to want is affordable fuel—just so long as it's produced in and transported through somebody else's back yard. That's often unfair.

Longer term, as a society, we've got to do a better job of setting priorities, and determining the cost-effectiveness of various options. We need good science, thorough testing, and sound, realistic public policies. Compliance costs must be considered in light of their impact on the cost of goods and services, on the nation's competitiveness, and especially on people's needs.

I think all of us can do a better job of this in the future:

- If society will take the care and the time to define the problems carefully.
- If industry, responsible environmental experts and the news media can create a greater public understanding of what causes pollution, and how it affects human health.
- If the government will avoid mandates and outright prohibitions, because very few issues are stark black-and-white.
- If the government will seek reasonable, meaningful standards and allow time for technology and innovation to achieve compliance. Solutions must be tested to see if they work and are cost-effective—and government should consult with a broader spectrum of people, including industry, before making rules, not after the fact. That puts the final decision in the hands of all of us as consumers, who ultimately must pay for the choices, and live with the consequences.
- And finally, we can better meet society's environmental and energy needs if we attack the problems together, and not as adversaries.

I'm optimistic. We've made a lot of progress in just a few years toward reconciling our needs for affordable energy and a clean environment. But this is a crucial point in the earth's environmental and economic history. The times demand leadership and courage. We have the opportunity to determine the course of history—the very future of planet Earth. If we don't respond to that opportunity—and do it now—future generations will not forgive us.

The pressures of regulation and litigation

The weight of regulations enacted by all levels of government—and the cost of litigation launched by government and by the privateers of the trial bar—have cumulatively risen to create an enormous cost burden on the U.S. economy.

Are we getting what we're paying for? We're not. And a key reason is that governmental decision-makers, and the courts, aren't in the habit of asking that question in the first place—of studying whether the benefits are worth the cost. In a sense they seem almost unaware that we're "paying" for regulation at all.

Government tends to concentrate on the benefits it is trying to achieve with a new regulation. The hoped-for benefits—environmental protection, safety on the highway, or whatever—are usually ones we can all embrace. But government's thinking processes don't necessarily recognize that there is also always a cost, and that when there are alternative ways of pursuing a particular societal objective we need strict cost/benefit analysis to help us understand which of those ways to choose.

It is, of course, simple common sense to spend money first where it will do the most good. By and large that is what the average consumer sets out to do with his or her own personal money. Government officials are just people, so there is no good reason government officials can't adopt that kind of common-sense attitude at work, too.

With that hope in mind, in 1993 I accepted an invitation to speak to the Program for Emerging Political Leaders given at the Darden Graduate School of Business Administration at the University of Virginia.

The audience was a group of younger officials who could be expected to make their marks in federal, state and local government for a long time to come. My remarks were intended to define the problem, and suggest solutions.

MILEPOST: JUNE 23, 1993

Striking the Balance Between the Costs and Benefits of Governmental Regulation

Darden Graduate School of Business Administration,
University of Virginia, Charlottesville

━━━━━━━━

One of the major jobs of a Chief Executive Officer today is creating and maintaining an open and honest relationship with the people who make and execute government policy—to work together with them, in a spirit of cooperation and collaboration, to serve the public.

Over the years, I've spent a great deal of my time doing just that, in this country and in many of the 150 countries where Texaco operates. It's generally been a pleasant experience for me. Certainly, it's always been a learning experience. And I believe it's been a good one for the public officials, as well. So I'm looking forward to spending this afternoon with you.

Talking about the issues of the time is particularly inspiring in this setting, here in what Thomas Jefferson called his "academical village." Walking among these buildings, across the great lawn and under the old trees, you can almost hear the voices of Jefferson and Madison and the others of that era, as they set the course of public policy that we still follow today.

It's not always an easy course—steering away from the rocks and shoals of misguided or extreme policies. Seeking to balance the powers of the state with the rights of the individual. Or trying to reconcile the need to encourage commerce and industry with the need to make sure that business fulfills its responsibilities to the public.

What is the role of government in all this? Mr. Jefferson, as they like to call him here in Charlottesville, once wrote that "the care of human life and happiness, and not their destruction, is the first and only legitimate object of good government." I think we can all agree with that.

But, that said, the going gets tougher. How do we best achieve that "care of human life and happiness"? How do we deploy society's resources most efficiently, to produce the greatest good for the greatest number?

That's the central question in the often difficult relationship between business and government. And it has been, for 200 years. It's the question I want to talk about today.

I've always thought it was a happy coincidence that, in the same year Thomas Jefferson wrote the Declaration of Independence, Adam Smith published *The Wealth of Nations*. Jefferson's was the ringing charter of political freedom—Smith's, the manifesto of economic freedom.

Smith described an economic system based on individual self-interest and regulated, not by government, but by what he realized was the "invisible hand" of supply and demand.

Both treatises were cut from the same cloth. And in the two centuries since, the pendulum of world events has swung back and forth between the extremes of rigid government control of the economy and the unfettered practice of capitalism.

At first, the pendulum's arc was wide. The gross abuses of early industrialization, during Dickens' time, provoked a reaction called Marxism. The gilded age of the Robber Barons led to the trust-busting of Teddy Roosevelt and the reforms of the Progressive era. Still later, the stock market excesses of the Roaring Twenties helped spawn the New Deal.

Each time, the pendulum's arc narrowed somewhat, as society adjusted to the Industrial Revolution. Then Communism—with its command-and-control mechanisms—collapsed.

Now we've come to a point in history where there seems to be a growing worldwide consensus about what works best in the economic sphere, and what doesn't. Where public leaders and business leaders can find common ground.

From my own experience, I'd describe the consensus this way: That the free-market system, while not perfect, is the best anyone's come up with so far for creating wealth, and thereby a rising standard of living for the most people. That it's the most effective because it best harnesses individual initiative and the awesome power of the human brain.

This consensus also recognizes the need for a reasonable amount of oversight of business by government, to prevent abuses and protect the public. And most business leaders would agree with that today.

Also part of this consensus is the recognition of government's strengths and limitations. That what government is best at, is doing the things that the people or the private sector cannot do for themselves. And what it is worst at is trying to do things best left to the private sector.

Now, despite this emerging consensus, there's still room for some honest differences of opinion. There remains a good deal of tension between business and government over exactly what their relationship ought to be—a tug-of-war over what best fills Mr. Jefferson's prescription for "the care of human life and happiness."

And certainly, some competitive tension is healthy, even desirable. But increasingly in recent years, it's starting to become evident to a lot of people in both business and government that this relationship could be less adversarial and more collaborative. Particularly when we face plenty of competition from outside our borders.

Forty years ago, when I was leaving the Navy and starting in business, we Americans didn't have to worry very much about that sort of thing. American economic power dominated the world. There was little competition from abroad. Jobs were plentiful, and the American worker was by far the highest paid in the world. The United States was routinely a net exporter, and federal surpluses were as common as deficits.

That's obviously all changed. Today, the American worker and American companies are in an economic barroom brawl with competitors from around the globe. Competition is white-hot, and getting hotter.

At the same time, the public's demands for government services, from highways to medical care, are rising exponentially. In fact, those demands are outstripping the economy's capacity to produce. So obviously, economic growth is vital to the continued health of our society.

As a result, we simply can no longer afford the amount of adversarial tension we've had between business and government in this country. The tug-of-war, instead of helping things, has become counter-productive.

In today's world, American business and government have to pull on the same end of the rope. We have to work for the same things.

And so, in my view, the time has come for a thorough re-examination of government's relation with business in this country, and the role of government regulation in fostering or impeding economic growth.

Now, as I said a moment ago, most reasonable people in business concede that a certain amount of government oversight is necessary, and in some cases, desirable.

However, the extension of government into virtually every corner of American life has become so pronounced in recent years that it is not simply a burden to big business. It's hurting everyone.

And here's the crux of my message: By slowing the engines of economic growth, the binge of regulations this country has been indulging itself in is wiping out existing jobs, choking off the creation of new ones, raising prices for the consumer, and making America less competitive in the world.

> **Regulation costs the American economy an estimated $400 to $500 billion a year.**

Now, I realize that a business leader talking about the burdens of government regulation is not a new phenomenon. But the news we read in the paper every day indicates the seriousness of the situation. As the sign in the Clinton election headquarters said: "It's the economy, stupid."

And it still is.

Today, regulation costs the American economy an estimated $400 to $500 billion a year. That's a hidden tax of roughly $4,000 to $5,000 annually for the average American family.

This country can no longer afford wasteful approaches to government regulation. Our resources are finite, and we have to allocate them wisely, to make our economy grow and remain competitive. We have to set priorities and make some hard choices. We just cannot afford to do everything we'd like to do, all at once, for environmental protection or any other public goal.

In fact, foolish and misguided regulations that sap economic growth are actually counter-productive. As the pollution problems in the former Soviet bloc attest, addressing environmental problems adequately requires the proper resources. And those resources depend on economic growth.

There's a further point: The litigation inspired by that tangle of regulations further saps America's competitiveness. Litigation adds a $150 billion burden to the U.S. economy. That may be a windfall for lawyers, but it doesn't do much for the average consumer.

You have to worry about a country that graduated 38,800 lawyers in 1991, and only 235 petroleum engineers.

You also have to worry about a country that, last year, for the first time ever, had more people working in civilian government jobs—federal, state and local—than in manufacturing jobs. How can we expect to compete with that sort of imbalance?

People like me, who have been talking about these issues long and often, have felt a bit like a voice crying in the wilderness.

Let me briefly summarize the several steps I urge legislators to consider before enacting new regulations:

> **New laws and regulations should be based on good science and thorough testing, rather than on the demands of the pressure groups that shout the loudest.**

First, subject all proposed legislation and regulations to some hard-nosed cost-benefit analysis. Society should try the least expensive methods first. And we ought to ask, just how much do we want to spend to remove that last billionth of a part of matter from the air or water? And could that money be spent more effectively elsewhere?

Second, new laws and regulations should be based on good science and thorough testing, rather than on the demands of the pressure groups that shout the loudest. On many issues, industry has a solid database that can provide guidance in writing regulations.

Third, consult with those affected, such as business leaders and consumers, before you impose new regulations. We can help, and we want to help, to find the best ways to achieve society's goals. We in the oil industry, for example, have a century's worth of experience in successfully providing energy society needs at an affordable price. We have an extensive infrastructure in place. And we have sophisticated technology that's breaking new ground every day.

Fourth, if we've learned anything in the past decade, it's that command-and-control approaches to the economy just don't work. Instead of dictating solutions and having bureaucrats micro-manage them, it's far better to let government set the standards to be met, and then leave it to marketplace forces and technology to figure out the best way to meet those standards. That puts the final decisions in the hands of consumers, who must pay for them.

■ Finally, we can all listen to one another a little more, and respect the other person's point of view—business people, government officials, opinion leaders, environmentalists, concerned private citizens. If reasonable people work together in a spirit of good will, I believe they can reach reasonable solutions.

I am convinced that we have the brains and the resources to significantly reduce unnecessary regulatory costs in this country. And we can do it without diminishing the nation's commitment to attaining worthwhile social gains. All we need is the resolve.

The American people need someone in their corner, to help strike an affordable balance between legitimate regulatory needs and economic growth. Achieving that, in my view, would be political leadership of the first order.

■

8

The Relentless Challenge of New Technology

One key to success in business or in any career path is the ability to adapt to innovation and new technologies—to see them as opportunities that lead to new breakthroughs and new growth for yourself and for your company, rather than as a misfortune that will leave you behind. This is a particular challenge for the CEO, who must lead in a technological environment that will have changed significantly, and often several times over, since he or she began his career.

But rapid technological change is not a new dilemma, no matter how many stories we read in the popular press about this being a time of unprecedented change.

Consider, for example, the events during the lifespan of one man, my grandfather, who died in 1922. During that single lifetime, the world's first oil well was completed (in 1859, the year of his birth), and the transcontinental railroad became a reality. These were followed by the electric light, the telephone and the phonograph in the 1870s. The first gasoline and diesel engines came in the 1880s, the first radio transmission in the 1890s, and the first airplane flight in 1903. My grandfather's life saw three major wars, three presidential assassinations and several financial panics. Men and women of his era were clearly called upon to understand and assimilate technological innovations that dramatically changed what their parents may well have thought were the immutable conditions of human life.

Or consider the impact of technology on the seemingly mundane industry of merchandising.

In our nation's early history, our largely rural population didn't go to stores. The stores came to the people, in the form of door-to-door peddlers. (Until the 1850s, in fact, peddler was the fourth-largest occupation in the United States, after farmer, planter and fisherman.) Then in 1886, a Minnesota farmer's son named Richard Warren Sears began selling watches by mail order. In short order he was selling everything from lingerie to washing machines—using the technology of postal rail freight to supplant the peddler's wagon and saddlebags. His innovation brought an undreamed-of wealth of consumer goods to the rural population, while simultaneously leveraging the size of this market to force enormous reductions in prices. All across rural America the arrival by mail of the Sears, Roebuck or Montgomery Ward catalogues—the "wish books," as they came to be known—was an event that young and old alike fondly anticipated each season.

In the growing cities and towns, meanwhile, most stores were located in the central business district, where customers reached them by trolley, horse-drawn vehicle or (heaven forbid!) by foot. But then the widespread availability of the automobile in the early half of this century began to change these buying habits, too. With the car, shoppers found they could reach a wider number of shopping areas— but they also found that they needed a place to park. In the late 1920s the visionary president of Sears, General Robert E. Wood, put these concepts together and came up with a revolutionary idea: retail stores outside the central business district, in locations that had adequate parking. The shopping center was born; and to this day his model sustains by far the largest share of our retail economy.

General Wood, by the way, was not a very good driver, and he was an even worse mechanic. But he understood change and he foresaw the impact of the automobile and the evolving demographic patterns on American consumers as no one had before him. He knew what he needed to know about technology, and he used his ideas to change the face of American retailing. His is a story of innovation every bit as impressive as, say, today's on-line petfood-dot-com.

It was also technology that enabled huge changes in where people live and how they make their living. What was once a nation of farmers now devotes only about 3 percent of its workforce to agriculture and food processing—yet this 3 percent is able to feed not only the U.S. but much of the rest of the world, through the technologies of farm equipment, fertilizer, pest control, improved strains of seed and the scientific practice of crop rotation. Similarly, the fractional horsepower electric motor replaced human muscle power with stators and rotors, which extended the industrial revolution into the house—which helped free women to pursue careers outside the home.

And each new technology tends to create its own new industry, which creates even more social change. Automobiles, airplanes, radios and telephones, electric motors and lights all spawned new companies and industries, each of them with a profound impact on our lifestyle. The new industries led to new forms of business organization—such as the mega-corporation, born in 1901 with the formation of U.S. Steel, and the assembly-line manufacturing system conceived by Henry Ford in 1913.

Now the information technology industry is having the same kind of impact, both because of the size and importance of the industry itself, and because of the way it is making it possible for management structures in all other industries to become flatter, more interactive and more efficient.

You hear criticism of the younger generation for relying too much on computers and other electronic wizardry. But not from me. I remember a time when low-tech was high-tech, and the high-tech of my day—a slide rule—was a great asset in my education.

In the 1930s, arithmetic was taught by rote and the basic tools were a pencil and some paper. Addition, subtraction, short division, multiplication, long division, squares and square roots were followed by the study of logarithms. And here came my first exposure to that fine example of technology: the slide rule.

A slide rule is basically a mechanical device to add and subtract logarithms. But to the youthful me, it was also a mysterious window into the future. I started with a simple one, but at age 14 I sent away for a Keuffel and Esser log log duplex trig model at the then extravagant price of $15. It was about a foot long and an inch and a half wide. It had a smooth slide that I made even silkier by the application of talcum powder (even then, improving technology provided a competitive advantage). Carrying this state-of-the-art device made me look like the '40s equivalent of today's nerd, but I loved it. The slide rule served me well through a succession of very competitive schools, and today sits on my desk for occasional use, and to terrify young assistants, reminding them that there was life before Intel.

The key point is, business executives must be comfortable with the technology of their day. Companies that ignore or resist change are doomed to failure. Those that reluctantly accept new methods and new technologies may be able to stay in business. But the greatest success will come to those who truly look over the horizon, grasp the potential of the new technology, and use it to go where none have gone before.

The corporate leader does not need to be at the leading edge of technical knowledge. But he or she needs to be conversant enough with the technology to be able to discuss it, to ask questions about it and, most importantly, to pick managers and programs that will contribute to the company's long-term success. Not all research projects will work out; the leader must know enough to decide which ones to feed and which ones to discontinue. The leader must choose the balance between short-term product improvement and longer-term fundamental innovation; it is this balance that will weigh most critically in the company's continued success.

New technology can be scary. But that's good. The best managers won't be those who are "comfortable" with the new paradigms—because comfort implies self-satisfaction. Better to be among those who are never satisfied.

In April of 1996, I was invited to the Darden Graduate School of Business Administration at the University of Virginia to address the topic, "what does today's CEO need to know about technology?"

The invitation was an intimidating one, in a sense, because it came from somebody who was well-qualified to answer that question himself: Thomas McAvoy. A professor at Darden, he had formerly served as the president and chief technology officer of Corning Inc.—a firm that has been re-inventing itself for 150 years. Thomas Edison invented the electric light bulb, but Corning made it. Corning spent money developing optical wave guides for 20 years before they were a commercial success; today these fibers make possible the Internet. Corning has demonstrated a unique ability to develop profitable commercialization of its research. It was thus with some trepidation that I addressed Dr. McAvoy's class.

MILEPOST: APRIL 19, 1996

The CEO's Role
in Technological Change

Darden Graduate School of Business Administration,
University of Virginia, Charlottesville, Virginia

Innovation is important in *all* businesses—not just the oil business, or Silicon Valley companies, or others that might immediately come to mind.

Certainly, it's more obvious in businesses such as drugs and automobiles, where continual innovation—particularly technological innovation—is integral to success. But the need to innovate is also important in other businesses, where change may be subtler. That's because, in even the most mundane industry, a company's attitude toward innovation can determine both its ability to discern the changes coming over the horizon, and its willingness to respond to them.

Look at merchandising — not ordinarily an industry you'd associate with innovation. But many of the old-line leaders have failed or are in trouble today—K-Mart, Montgomery Ward and Caldor. Even Sears has had to take heroic measures to regain its past position of leadership.

Business has been lost to companies that took more innovative approaches to determining and satisfying customer preferences, such as mail order, and in low-cost computer-driven applications, which minimize or eliminate inventories.

Another example is laundry detergents—hardly what one thinks of as a high-tech business. But 50 years ago, Procter and Gamble developed the first synthetic detergent—Tide. It was an enormous technical innovation in 1946. More important, its impact is still being felt today. Because P&G used the Tide technology as the starting point to develop both improved formulations and other brands. And it became the catalyst for transforming the company into today's household products giant and the world's biggest advertiser.

In the business that I know best, the oil industry, the need for innovation is obvious. And there are many ways to use innovation to create new value: to develop new products and manufacturing processes, to come up with new services, to improve your marketing. Reformulated gasoline, on-site vapor recovery and card-reading pumps come to mind.

But it is most important in exploring for and developing new sources of petroleum. Because value in the oil business has traditionally been added by finding and producing oil and natural gas.

Worldwide, the industry has done a pretty good job of that over the past 25 years. That's why, when you adjust for inflation, the price of gasoline in this country today is as low as it's been since they started to keep track of it, in 1920.

And it's why gasoline, fuel oil and the industry's other products are universally available in plentiful quantities. That's in spite of several Mideast oil crises, price controls in the U.S., the Persian Gulf War, and the need for significant reductions in automobile and other sources of pollution.

Back in the 1970s, experts were predicting the demise of petroleum as the world's primary source of energy. They said that crude oil prices would rise to $50 or $60 or more. Others believed that world oil reserves would dry up in 50 years. Some were even proposing installing thousands of windmills across the land, to replace oil, either because sources of oil would dry up, or because they thought that oil couldn't satisfy environmental demands.

They were all wrong. Today, oil is selling on world markets for about $20 per barrel. Oil and gas provide roughly 60 percent of the world's energy. And over the past 20 years, global reserves have been increased by 60 percent—even though worldwide annual consumption has risen 36 percent.

Looking ahead, the world has at least a 50-year supply of oil and gas, and we continue to add to our reserve base all the time. And I don't see too many windmills being built.

How did we do it? How did we confound the doomsayers and defy the so-called experts? Largely through innovation, particularly technological innovation.

In the oil industry, the impact of technology has been most dramatic in helping us find and produce oil and gas economically. "Economically" is the key word here.

The common measure of success we use is reserve replacement. In other words, how much of the oil and gas we pumped out of the ground in the past year were we able to able to replace by finding additional reserves?

Reserve replacement is a point of great pride with most oil people. But almost anyone can replace reserves at least temporarily by throwing money at the job. The challenge is to do it profitably, and create value for shareholders. That means keeping our finding and development costs under control. And it means balancing the risk profile of our investments to optimize our results.

And doing all this requires the full commitment of the chief executive officer.

During my tenure as CEO, we added two dollars in proven reserves for every one dollar we spent on exploration and development. That was among the best performances of the major oil companies.

And we did it with several techniques. Let me tell you about them.

First, one must understand the technology being used to find and produce oil and gas economically. Some of it is truly amazing.

A major example is three-dimensional seismic imaging. Here, high-pressure compressed air guns send pulses of energy into the earth's surface. The reverberations are recorded by hydrophones attached to cables pulled over seas by boats, or placed at intervals on land. From these results, we can construct computerized models that let geo-scientists actually "see" into the earth below, to find hydrocarbon deposits.

> **Almost anyone can replace reserves by throwing money at the job. The challenge is to do it profitably.**

But seismic surveys are expensive and time-consuming. Now, our scientists have developed vertical cable seismic, where engineers attach hydrophones to cables that are then planted vertically, with one end attached to the sea floor. That cuts costs dramatically and improves resolution.

Another exciting new technology is salt proximity testing. This allows oil companies to image under salt domes economically for the first time. Salt is resistant to seismic imaging, but often exists over deposits of oil and gas. In the Gulf of Mexico, we have scheduled well testing to evaluate substantial oil and gas reservoirs found beneath 2,900 feet of salt.

Once oil or gas has been found, there are new technological advances to help get more of it out of the ground. One of these is horizontal drilling. Here, engineers drill down, then actually turn the drill bit gradually, until it's boring horizontally through the oil-bearing strata. This exposes a lot more oil to the production casing.

Oil companies are also using enhanced oil recovery to increase production. This entails injecting steam, water, CO_2, or other materials into the ground to loosen viscous oil and force more oil or gas toward the well bore. This helps us retrieve more reserves economically—even low-grade, bottom-of-the-barrel oil that otherwise would not be cost-effective to produce.

Rapid developments in advanced technology are also making oil and gas production economically possible from areas where we could not go before. In 1984, we participated in bringing on-stream Green Canyon 184 in the Gulf of Mexico, in 1,800 feet of water.

It was a technical success, but never did generate a book profit, because unit costs were too high, based on production techniques available 10 year ago.

Now however, we can produce profitably in even deeper water by using subsea completions and other technological advances. Subsea completions, which companies are also using in the North Sea, involve installing pumps and manifolds on the ocean floor, and then piping the oil and gas back as much as 50 or 60 miles, to existing facilities in shallower water.

Deepwater technology is advancing so fast that Texaco and three other companies are now planning to drill a wildcat well in 7,800 feet of water—one and a half miles—in the Gulf of Mexico.

So technology has opened new areas to oil and gas productions, and made older areas more attractive. The question for top management is: How do you choose among them?

The trick is to balance your investments, to optimize results. And that may be as much an art as a science; as much gut feeling as financial analysis.

From my experience, I believe there are three ways to achieve that balance and optimization:

- Discipline in allocating capital.
- Allocation of adequate funds for research.
- And cost control.

Let me elaborate.

First, discipline in allocating capital. Here, the challenge is not to be dazzled by all the opportunities and fantastic technology, like a kid in a candy store. Not to end up chasing some will o'the wisp.

In the oil industry, discipline means designing an exploration program with an appropriate balance of risk. You need a portfolio of opportunities of different sizes, different locations, different degrees of risk.

Certainly, rank wildcatting is the most exciting part of exploration. But 90 percent of wildcats are likely to be failures. And spending all of your money on a hunt for elephants—those rare enormous finds that come along infrequently—might bring you headlines. But it carries the risk of economic disaster. On the other hand, a succession of small and sure discoveries may produce a high success rate, but may not produce large profits. The best approach is to hedge your bets, by balancing large and small projects, risky and less risky.

It is also the general practice in the oil industry today to spread the risk by entering into partnerships with other companies. This lets you put more bets on more prospects.

As one successful old wildcatter once told me, "I'd rather have a one-eighth interest in a gusher than own 100 percent of a dry hole." That makes a lot of sense.

Allocating adequate funds for research in exploration and production is the second method of balancing your investments and optimizing results. We can make money from research. I've often said that in the oil business, we can find as much oil in the laboratory as in the oil field.

Not too many years ago, recovering 20 percent or less of the oil and gas trapped in a reservoir was standard. But today's technology has allowed us to double or triple the percentage of oil and gas recovered. Drilling techniques and enhanced recovery projects are the keys here.

The third way to improve your investments and optimize results is through cost control. This requires good planning, and solid organization to carry those plans through.

In the oil industry, the trick is to analyze finding and lifting costs, and see what changes can be made to reduce costs. Here, technology can play a major role. For example, by computerizing our fields, to automate the control operations of our pumping units, we can reduce power and maintenance costs. The subsea completions I mentioned earlier also make production from remote offshore areas profitable, because they allow us to pipe the oil and gas back to existing platforms, thus saving the enormous cost of building additional offshore platforms.

A consulting group recently studied the industry and deter-mined the characteristics of companies that are economically successful in oil exploration and production. The results are not surprising. In fact, they apply to most industries: oil companies successful in exploration and production have access to a high level of technology. In addition, they are organized and man-aged well:

- They have flat, lean organizations. Those organizations are generally based on teams.
- Their managements focus on results, not process. Decision-making authority is pushed down in the organization.
- They have established performance measurement systems.
- And management has a clear understanding of the com-pany's core competencies and a strategy designed to exploit them.

In addition, the oil industry has some additional hallmarks of success as it deals with some special challenges.

Because we must go where the oil is, the oil industry is more vulnerable than many to uncontrollable outside events, like wars or natural disasters. But good planning and foresight can mini-mize the effects of even those disasters.

And because we have to go farther and farther afield as nearby oil is depleted, the oil industry also must invest its resources in areas that are often politically or geographically hostile, or at least difficult.

For example, the countries of the former Soviet Union have enormous potential reserves. But Western companies' progress in tapping those reserves has come in fits and starts, due to the political changes in those countries, their lack of physical and legal infrastructure, and the other problems inherent in moving into the strange—to them—new world of free enterprise.

Now, what is the CEO's role in all this? Obviously, the CEO does do a great deal, in coordination with the top management team, to set the overall tone of the organization—by defining the cor-porate culture, encouraging the right kind of behavior, spotting and nurturing talent, and setting overall strategy.

But equally important in a capital-intensive business like oil is allocating capital investments. Determining what to do — where best to deploy the company's technological resources.

And how to do it? Determining the most advantageous tim-ing, how much risk is appropriate and so forth. And knowing when to raise the stakes and when to fold your cards and re-direct the company's efforts.

In making these determinations, the CEO and the rest of the top management team have to grow the business, by investing in projects that make a cash return in an acceptable time period. That's important.

But that doesn't mean neglecting the long term. Not all research or investment can—or should—have an immediate economic benefit. Certainly, every CEO wants to maximize the current year's profits. But the top job also carries with it a sound and careful stewardship of the company and its future.

The CEO must operate with that in mind. For a number of reasons. It reassures customers that the company's products or services are produced with an eye toward long-term dependability. It is hard evidence for Wall Street of management's faith in the company's future. And it demonstrates to the company's employees their management's commitment to the future. This encourages an optimism and commitment that's healthy and infectious. That not only attracts and keeps the best talent. It also inspires the very kind of innovative behavior a leading company needs.

> **The finest legacy of a CEO is how well the company does after he or she leaves.**

For those reasons, I believe the finest legacy of a CEO is how well the company does after he or she leaves.

Perhaps the best illustration of this point I can think of involves Professor McAvoy. When Tom was research chief at Corning, he was the leading proponent of developing fiber optics. And for years, Corning spent money on them. But the company's CEO believed in fiber optics. And he believed in what Tom and his team were doing.

Today, of course, our worldwide communications system would not be possible without fiber optics, and they are an enormously profitable business for Corning.

No CEO is omniscient, of course. He is only as good as the facts and information he gets from his organization.

So it's important that individual employees feel free to give you the bad news, along with the good. And to tell you when they think that you're off-base.

In this regard, how detailed a knowledge of the technology must the CEO possess? Most CEOs cannot be totally up-to-date and conversant with all of the engineering details. But they should know the vocabulary, know the theory, and know what they don't know, so that they can ask the important, relevant questions.

Now once you, as a CEO, are armed with the very best information you can get, you still come face-to-face with the stark reality that, in the final analysis, only you can make the big decisions. And ultimately, you are responsible for the results.

That's when it's time to look out the window, or in the mirror, or maybe at the picture of your family on your desk, and bring to the job what only you can provide—your intelligence, your experience, your wisdom, your courage. Things you can find only inside yourself.

If you've had good advice from your people, that will be easier. But the buck still stops with the CEO. And proper allocation of investment capital, research effort, and exploration expense remain the most important areas for an oil company CEO to exercise his final authority.

He reviews the facts, uses his judgment, makes the decision—and prays for a bit of good luck!

9

With Affection:
Taking a Role with
Not-for-Profits

Americans are the most generous people in the history of the world. This tradition dates to our earliest days as a nation, when the doctrine of the separation of church and state both allowed and required our ancestors to maintain their own churches at their own expense. The churches were followed by the establishment of private colleges, by hospitals, and eventually by a huge array of charitable institutions devoted to preserving and improving human life.

Today over 2.1 percent of the United States' GDP is contributed annually by Americans to not-for-profit groups. The not-for-profit sector—the fifth estate, if you will—plays a vital role in our economy and culture, and is a major force for good. Free from governmental interference, and supported by private donations, not-for-profits are a key source of innovation and ideas in our effort to build a better society.

Business executives are often called upon to play a role in the not-for-profit arena, and the best ones find that this is not so much an obligation as an opportunity. Charity work affords both active and retired executives an opportunity to take on new challenges, to learn about people and problems they might not encounter in their ordinary business life, to make new contacts and to learn new skills—all while satisfying the basic human need to make a contribution.

Not-for-profit work is something for which executives from the for-profit world are eminently qualified. For the most part they have the financial wherewithal. By definition they have organizational experience. And they have the inner drive to make a difference in whatever they do.

Service on a not-for-profit board must be taken very seriously. Audit, investment and nominating committees, for example, are just as important to the health of these groups as they are to the health of for-profit businesses—and similar care must be taken. Service on a not-for-profit board is not a social stepping-stone; it is a serious opportunity to perform for the public good, and it deserves the best effort we can bring to it.

To succeed in business you must meet the needs of your customers for goods and services; in the not-for-profit world you succeed only if people donate money to the cause of their own volition. So fundraising is a crucial task—and requires skills that even the most successful and experienced business executives may have to learn afresh.

Many people shy away from the task of asking others for money. But in doing so they miss the feeling of satisfaction that accompanies a successful fundraising effort.

Giving money to worthwhile causes is, I have learned, often a source of great happiness to the giver. So the successful fundraiser must be convinced himself that this particular activity is important and necessary; that's the key to bringing pleasure to the donor and the donee alike. If the organization is seen to be productive and well-run, then adequate contributions, whether for annual giving or for endowment, should be achievable.

But service on a not-for-profit's board involves responsibilities beyond fundraising. Raising money is one thing; investing and spending it is something else again.

When dealing with other people's money one must be very careful. The tendency in not-for-profits is to take a very conservative investment approach, sacrificing return for "safety." A more productive approach is the creation of an adequate endowment fund to provide a safety net so that investments can be made for the longer term, with no less than a market return. The successful not-for-profit boards do not spend money before they have raised it; they have the fiscal discipline to conduct their major fundraising before the cornerstones are laid.

Whether in medicine, education or the arts, not-for-profits often have excellent professional staffs, who have detailed expertise and selfless devotion to their calling. They know more about the technology and the practice of their specialties than most board members could ever hope to achieve. These professionals are dedicated, hardworking, idealistic people who devote their lives to the service of *pro-bono* causes. Some professional staffs do, however, have a tendency to create administrative overburden, and over time put their own directional spin on the organization. It is the responsibility of the not-for-profit board, therefore, to guide the organization toward its selected goal, to set objectives, to gauge progress against these objectives, and to keep costs under control.

These basic approaches have worked well in a variety of institutions: cultural, medical and educational. A case in point is St. Paul's School, a co-educational boarding school serving the 9th through the 12th grades. St. Paul's was founded in Concord, New Hampshire, in 1846, and today has 500 students of very diverse backgrounds from all over the United States and from overseas. St. Paul's is a Christian school with an Episcopalian tradition, but it admits students of all faiths. Over the years its graduates have distinguished themselves in the law, government, medicine, business, the arts, and the military.

Service for 19 years on St. Paul's board, 12 of them as president of the board, provided me with an excellent opportunity to be of service in the area of secondary education—an important cause, in my view, because what takes place during the formative years is the incubator for so much later success.

Besides the practical experience it provided, service on this board offered other rewards. During some very troubled times at Texaco, when it seemed that whatever could go wrong did go wrong, the Rector of St. Paul's School, the Reverend Charles H. "Kelly" Clark, used to call regularly to offer his support. One Friday afternoon of a particularly trying week Kelly asked, "Jim, what can I do for you?" My answer: "Kelly, let's try prayer; I've tried every other damn thing." The efficacy of this suggestion speaks for itself.

Not only was he good in dealing with Higher Authority, Kelly was also very good with the world around him—and the environmental and societal challenges it presents. These challenges once took the form of a pair of beavers who spent the spring felling a large number of beautiful trees all around the lovely Lower School pond. Students can become instantly and emotionally attached to animals—particularly if said animals are seen as presenting a problem for adult authority. After a long trustees meeting at which various options were discussed, Kelly simply said, "summer vacation is soon to be here. The students will return in the fall, but the beavers will not." The solution was humane, but effective.

A more important question confronting the St. Paul's board during the 1980s was the idea of a new library. Was it needed? How could we pay for it? Where to build it? Would it work? We confronted those questions, and more. The dedication ceremony for the new library afforded an opportunity to reflect on the answers.

MILEPOST: APRIL 21, 1991

Love and Labor in a Good Cause

St. Paul's School Library Dedication, Concord, New Hampshire

I am so proud of what has happened today and what continues to happen in the life and times of St. Paul's School.

The love and the labor of many cannot be better illustrated than by the existence of our beautiful new library. Tonight, I'm going to try to recognize the many, and I'm going to tell you a little bit about the labor by which this library has become reality.

I think an understanding of the process is particularly important because, let's face it, it cost a lot of money. And when you are a Trustee and you commit the funds of others, you have a significant responsibility. One can spend one's own money as one likes; that's obvious. Spending someone else's takes very, very special care. And the creation of a large and enduring structure is a somewhat irreversible action that must be done right the first time.

Now you can argue about how long ago the idea of the library was generated. You can see some early designs from 1895. But in fact, the real idea for this library originated here at the School within the last ten years. The School knew, in its wisdom, that we needed a new library.

An idea, in St. Paul's School or any other institution, needs a champion. Committees are useful and I'm going to talk more about committees in a moment. And they were used. But individuals have ideas. Individuals champion causes. Individuals cause events to happen.

There were a number of options, and in this, as in any other sort of thing, we had the "do-nothing" option. And since we'd done nothing in one sense since 1901, I guess we could have done nothing for a while longer. But our intent was for St. Paul's School to be the best in this area, as in every other area. So we asked ourselves, what is the best? It's clear that library science in the future is going to consist of more than microfiche and magnetic tape and a few of these CRTs. Will computer technology be the heart of the future library? That had to be studied, as did a number of other things.

As you heard today, we considered expanding Sheldon.* We gave that idea a good college try. It didn't work; it didn't provide what we wanted. Sheldon is a beautiful building. We didn't want to tear it down. It has beautiful architecture. We talk about that as Flagg's example of Classical Revival; that's what Bob Stern** calls it. As rather irreverent students, we called it "The Inkwell." I'm sure nobody calls it that anymore, but I know we did.

This study then led us to the decision to build anew. And that led us to the vision of Robert Stern. You saw that vision demonstrated well today in one of the greatest *tours de force* that I have ever seen. The man is a genius, and he has given his genius to us in the form of our new library.

Now, he passed over, a little bit, some of the serious discussion of where we were going to put our new library. One of the places he wanted to put it was down in that meadow. I can tell you, when I was a V Former here, I built a raft to sail down the Sluice— I'm a sailor anyhow. And most of us know that the Sluice can rise ten feet about its banks in the springtime and flood that meadow. So that really wasn't a very good place to put the library.

We looked at the hill up there behind Drury. We looked at the Golf Course. And then we looked at the Lower School Pond, more or less in the area where the school's original home stood. When I was here as a boy, the site was covered with buildings that are now gone. This was the perfect place, to be at the center of this archetypal New England village that we call St. Paul's School.

On the other hand, you know anything that happens at St. Paul's once becomes a tradition. Some of the masters here will understand what I mean. And our new generation has a tradition of playing Frisbee out where we were going to put the library. And they said, "You can't put a library out there. You're going to interfere with the Frisbee games."

Well, we considered that, and we figured there were other places for Frisbee. And in fact, there are.

The new library was also going to eliminate the Community Center. But the student enthusiasm for a new Community Center

---

* *The existing library.*

** *The distinguished architect Robert A.M. Stern, who designed the new library.*

was very high, indeed. So we built a new one, and it's lighter and less threatening. It's no longer the Black Hole of Calcutta, and thus has become an instant success with the Trustees. One can hope that in future years it may also earn a feeling of warmth in the hearts of the students—but it's too early to say that!

Now let's talk about the library. In my career I've done a lot of big construction, and one of the things I always ask when I get started is, "Will it work?" It's wonderful to have good materials, good construction, and beauty, but you ask yourself, "Will it work?" In the case of the library, what do I mean by "Will it work?"

Well, you think about traffic flow and acoustics and the heights of tables and chairs, and modern electronics, the lighting, the comfort, the heating, ventilating, air conditioning, what you do about muddy feet, and what you do about antique volumes. In other words, "Will it work?"

And I can tell you today that the library does work. I have seen it. I have watched it. The library is truly a working storehouse of information. In addition, not as an oversight, the materials and the artistic content of that library are superb.

> **This Board has one great policy, and that is, we don't spend money we don't have.**

We didn't fool around with planning forever. It just seemed like forever. But we voted in April of '87 to proceed. The ground was broken in June of '88. We explained it to the school family in New York in February of '89. Cornerstone in 1990. The books went in by human conveyor in January of this year. So, that is a little of the mechanical process by which it was built.

But how do you finance it? You know, you're talking about a lot of money. And this Board has one great policy, and that is, we don't spend money we don't have.

We set out to describe the project, to create the case, and to raise the money. And I will tell you something about the family of St. Paul's School. When they understand the case, they are incredibly generous.

Thanks to the Trustees, thanks to the ever-generous alumni.

Then there was the question: how to construct it? It was constructed well, with bids and a cap on the changes and scope, the right choice of materials, and sound foundations, site borings to make sure that it will not fall. And of all these things, our Vice Rector was the czar. At the end of the day, when you're building something, you have to have a czar. You have to have absolute control over scope changes. (I hear my wife giggling, because we don't have that at our house. There's no control at all there over scope changes.) But in big construction, you have to have discipline. The Vice Rector provided the discipline, and the project was brought in on budget.

Why do we have a library? What do we need it for?

It is perhaps unlikely that the prayers that are said in the beautiful confines of the Chapel of St. Peter and St. Paul are more likely to be answered than those said anywhere else. I would suggest, however, that it is possible that those devotions are more likely to occur in those inspiring surroundings.

Similarly, we look at the beautiful Performing Arts Center. It has obviously raised our production of very, very splendid ballet dancers. We have our new laboratory that houses Dr. Enders' Nobel medal. That has clearly increased the number of our engineering aspirants. We look at the Rectory, that marvelous Victorian building, as a symbol of the family of St. Paul's School. There is a family feeling that has been created by Kelly and Priscilla Clark in that marvelous house. The structure, so lovingly lived in, tells an important story. And for this, we are particularly grateful to Priscilla, who has filled this house with the aura of love.*

I'll tell you a little personal story. Twice in my life I've had the privilege of visiting the Church of Mary Magdalene in Vezelay, France. This church began in 860. I think they'll never finish it, and they were still working on it in the 1800s. It rises on a hill of a thousand feet over the plains of central France. And you can see, as you look at this church, the entire history of medieval architecture, from the Romans to the Romanesque to Gothic architecture. You can also see the aspirations and the hopes and achievements and the faith of the people who have lived in that little village. You know, if you study it, that St. Bernard incited the Second Crusade in that church. And you also know that Richard the Lionhearted and Philip II of France planned the Third Crusade right there in that church.

So think about that. Ask what is the potential impact of this library on the life of St. Paul's School? Is it possible that we

---

* As mentioned above, the Reverend Charles "Kelly" Clark was Rector of St. Paul's School; Priscilla is Mrs. Clark.

shall have St. Bernard and perhaps Richard the Lionhearted over there, planning their next crusade? Knowing St. Paul's as well as I do, I would not bet against it. I think that great people will plan great events in the building that we have provided for them. And, to quote one of my heroes in this world, Winston Churchill, "We shape our buildings; thereafter, they shape us."

Certainly, we believe that this library will be encouragement for academic excellence. It will provide instant availability of the wisdom of the ages. It will provide for serious interchange of ideas among our students and faculty, and perhaps a little handholding on the side. It is a totally wonderful and beautiful building.

So, to end as I began. I want to give thanks to those who made it possible. To our wonderful Board of Trustees as a group. To all the thousands of donors. And clearly, and very, very sincerely, to Kelly and Priscilla for their leadership in this, as in every venture of this School. And to you all, I thank you.

10

When the Time Comes to Move On

The last thing a CEO does for his or her company is in many ways the most important—that is, ensuing an orderly departure and a strong succession.

This is a task that must begin years in advance of your actual departure, with the identification and then the grooming of possible successors. Successors should be trained not only in the whys and wherefores, the nuts and the bolts of the business. They should also have the experience of semi-autonomous leadership, to both develop and test their self-reliance and their people skills.

Only a constant testing of decision-making and personal relationships over an extended period of time will identify those best qualified for ultimate leadership. Real leadership requires good ideas, and the ability to convince others that they really are good ideas; no matter how visionary the leader, he governs best who succeeds in having his visions shared. This combination of qualities in a potential successor will not emerge unless you take the time for the new leadership to become aware of the new responsibilities, and for the organization to become accepting of the new boss.

The outgoing CEO must train and test potential successors, and must recommend the ultimate successor to the company's board of directors, in ample time to leave at the mandatory retirement age with the company in good hands. And then the outgoing CEO should really, genuinely leave. Succeeding managements must be able to use their training and experience to do their very best, taking full responsibility for their actions unfettered by second-guessing from their predecessors.

It may seem superficially attractive to retain the former CEO in service on the board, but in most cases that doesn't turn out to be productive. Times change, people change, new opportunities appear, and a new generation of business management should be ready and empowered to confront the future. Institutional memory is important; as George Santayana said, "those who cannot remember the past are condemned to repeat it." But a former CEO can hold himself ready to offer advice—to help his successors understand the errors and triumphs of the past—without clutching the authority invested in a board seat.

None of this means, of course, that it is easy to turn over the leadership to someone else, no matter how qualified and how trusted. I guess that if one didn't miss the job of CEO, one should not have had it in the first place. I've often been asked if I miss it, and the honest answer is, yes, I miss the excitement, the challenges, the sense of duty, and the opportunity to effect positive change.

Interestingly, the thoughts and concerns that come to mind on approaching the end of a career in active business management can be remarkably similar to those that occupy one's head at the beginning. There's the expectation of a new lifestyle to come. You feel fear of the unknown, and trepidation over the coming changes. But there's also anticipation of new ways to use one's talents, choices to be made—and a general conviction that, whatever happens, one will do one's best.

For there is life after CEO-dom. The same talents that made for success in direct business leadership are also badly needed in other areas. And even in retirement, any CEO will want a chance to deploy those talents.

Certainly the new retiree cherishes the time with family, the travel and recreation. Hobbies, sports and reading will all have hours available to them, which had been denied in the past. But hard as it may be to believe, there really is a limit to how many golf balls you can hit or how many fish you can catch. The brain, too, needs constant exercise to stay in shape.

A well-planned and productive retirement may include service on other corporate boards, where accumulated wisdom and experience can be put to good use. In addition, there is no shortage of opportunity to be of use in the not-for-profit world, as discussed in Chapter 9. You do not need to be a surgeon to make a worthwhile contribution to a hospital board. In the arts, someone who couldn't carry a tune in a bucket may nonetheless be able to make a contribution in a position of leadership. Investment, fundraising, salesmanship and planning expertise are all invaluable to the not-for-profit sector. So, too, will be your enthusiasm. And in my view, the rewards of success in the business world carry with them the responsibility to do *good*, as well as to do *well*.

As I neared my retirement from the company, I knew I would continue in outside activities that would engage my intellect and abilities. But that didn't prevent this from being an emotional time. The leader should be pardoned on this occasion if he allows a little of his soul to show through, as it did in this final milepost.

MILEPOST: MARCH 29, 1993

The CEO Says Farewell

The Texaco Round Table, White Plains, New York

It is good for us to be here in our beautiful auditorium on this my last day as an employee—and together we are going to have another wonderful day.

Think of the great events that you and I have shared in this room. You know they say that walls have ears. Well, I think perhaps the walls of this room have memories. They have memories of the great events that have taken place right here. Let's think about what some of those great events were.

I'll refer to our vision to be among the most admired companies in America. It was a long reach from a very low point. Outrageous? Of course, it was outrageous!

It was right here that we announced our declaration of Chapter 11— rather than submit to extortion and to the corruption of the Texas legal system. I will never forget walking in here that Monday morning, the 13th of April, and the standing ovation. That was really wonderful. That was what made it all possible.

Our settlement. I didn't get a standing ovation that day. I didn't want to settle that damn thing anyhow, as you probably know.

Our strategy to win a takeover battle. I remember standing right here; and we had about 200 people in this room. We were talking about how we were going to win that one. And we did!

And more recently, our plans and our planning process and our many security analyst meetings right here that have clearly established Texaco as a leader—or the leader—in the industry.

Our compact for education in the State of New York, when we shared this rostrum with Governor Mario Cuomo, to come up with a new way to improve the education and the life of the people in this state.

Our Toys for Tots program and our Christmas program with the stars from the Metropolitan Opera. To me, it's one of the high points of our year. I have always loved it, and I know that you have.

Many exciting speakers and our ever-improving video conferences, where we're using the technology of a modern world to communicate literally throughout the world of Texaco our ideas and plans for the future.

Yes, all these events tell the story that you and I know so well—how Texaco rediscovered its heritage and how it became once again the Tiffany of the oil industry.

So here we are. The past is only prologue. What do we do for an encore? We have proven that we can beat the competition. And if there were one thing that I say today that I hope you do remember, it is that beating the competition in the business in which we are involved is very, very important. And we have proven that we can do it. We must know the competition. We must know what they do, how they do it, and make sure that we do it better. And we have to do that every day of our lives because we are operating in the most competitive business in the world.

We have our new and our improved planning process. If I look at the five-year plan, it's very, very bright. I think it can be a lot better. I think that all of you can beat that plan. But the plan that we have in front of us now for the next five years shows a great five years to come.

Quality is a part of the Texaco life.

We have our quality process throughout the company. You know quality can become very complicated when you get into all the esoterics of it. To me, quality means being the best person that I can be. It encourages us all to be the best that we can be. It encourages teamwork, shared goals, hard work, and high ideals. Quality is a part of the Texaco life, and I want it to continue to be part of the Texaco life.

We are a company—you and I—we are a company that respects the individual, that encourages advancement on merit and solely on merit, a company where everyone, man and woman alike, can succeed to the very best of his or her ability, and where there are no bars of race or gender or color or creed or nationality. That is the company that we are and we must be.

Having said all that, I would remind you that change will continue to be the way of the future.

Texaco fell into the morass. That's a pretty good word. For those of you who remember that as do I, it was, in fact, a morass in the 1970s—because of an inability and unwillingness to see how the future would be different from the past. What had worked so well in the past really wasn't going to work very well into the future. It was no longer going to succeed, because of a belief that tomorrow would look very much like yesterday.

We cannot fear change. We must welcome it. We must understand that the mere existence of change gives us the chance to excel. If everything were frozen into place, we'd never have that chance. The existence of change and changing circumstances gives us the chance to prove again, probably every day, that we really are the best.

Those companies that have ignored these ideas have failed their employees, their customers, and their shareholders. Think about that for a moment. Those companies that have ignored these ideas have failed their employees, their customers, and their shareholders.

> **We cannot fear change. We must welcome it.**

Those companies who have adopted change as an ongoing process have succeeded over the years, and they have rewarded their employees with job growth, personal economic success, and the satisfaction that comes from serving with the very, very best. And they have rewarded their communities and their shareholders with growing investments, with dividends, and with stock appreciation.

We have in place a solid management team at all levels. My good friend of so many years, Al DeCrane, is a strong, experienced, and creative leader who is no stranger to the heat of the kitchen. We all remember Harry Truman—you know, "if you can't stand the heat, get out of the kitchen."

Al was right there with his big white hat on. He knows what the heat of the kitchen is all about. And he's still there.

He was a leader in each of the events of recent history, some of which I mentioned to you. He is a quality adherent in every sense of the word; and he is devoted personally and totally to your success and to that of the company.

Through our human resources committees, our quality program, we have created outstanding management throughout the company at every level and at every location. And I have every confidence in Al as our new CEO and the whole team to lead this company into the future.

Now after nearly 40 years with Texaco and eight years in the United States Navy before that, do I have any free advice to offer? You know I do. You have been getting my free advice for a long, long while. But here are some things I jotted down that might be useful.

Become a quality person eager to work to your fullest ability and eager to work with and help others. And that last phrase is a hallmark of Texaco, because one thing that I have always known and thought about Texaco people is that if you ask them for help, they are going to help you. So be eager to work with and to help others.

Set high goals for yourself and your organization. Goals of performance and goals of achievement will lead to goals of recognition.

Keep a smile on your face and optimism in your heart. Pessimism will guarantee failure. Now, optimism does not guarantee success, but it will certainly encourage success.

Read diverse and sometimes serious books. Read something other than the high school football scores. Read about history and art and biography and science and music. These kinds of pursuits expand the mind.

You know the genius of the human brain is beyond imagination. Give it a chance to work. Become an interesting person with an inquiring mind. And you can do that by expanding your horizons through the use of good literature.

Stay healthy. Don't eat too much; don't drink too much; get a little exercise from time to time; and find somebody to talk to. I think these are all elements of staying healthy.

And remember this: That Texaco's greatest successes lie in the future. Whatever we have achieved in the past is only important in that it allows us to be here today and to do great things into the future.

No road is straight. And you can be sure that there is a lion or a tiger around each corner. But you have proven that you have the right stuff to deal with those lions and those tigers that I know lie out ahead.

I thank you for your hard work, for your success, and most of all for your friendship. And if you remember me at all—and I sincerely hope that you do—I hope that it will be as a happy warrior who left the place at least somewhat better than he found it.

Thank you. Thank you, one and all.

Index